YOUR FAITHFUL BRAIN

IGNITED!

IGNITING THE HEART-BRAIN CONNECTION AT THE INTERSECTION OF FAITH & SCIENCE

Dondra Agovino, MAC, LPC & Gina Birkemeier, MAC, LPC
Foreword by Dr. Leonard Matheson

© 2019 Dondra Agovino and Gina Birkemeier

Your Faithful Brain . . . Ignited!
Igniting the Heart-Brain Connection at the Intersection of Faith & Science

First Edition, January 2019

Out Loud Publishing
St. Louis, MO.
itsmyoutloudvoice.com

Editing: Shayla Raquel, ShaylaRaquel.com
Publishing and Design Services: Melinda Martin, MelindaMartin.me

Your Faithful Brain . . . Ignited! Igniting the Heart-Brain Connection at the Intersection of Faith & Science is under copyright protection. No part of this book may be used or reproduced in any manner whatsoever without written permission except in the case of brief quotations embodied in critical articles and reviews. Printed in the United States of America. All rights reserved.

Scripture taken from The Voice™. Copyright © 2008 by Ecclesia Bible Society. Used by permission. All rights reserved.

THE HOLY BIBLE, NEW INTERNATIONAL VERSION®, NIV® Copyright © 1973, 1978, 1984, 2011 by Biblica, Inc.® Used by permission. All rights reserved worldwide.

ISBN 978-1-7329545-0-2 (paperback)

WELCOME!

Welcome to *Your Faithful Brain... Ignited!*, written by my close friends and colleagues Dondra Agovino and Gina Birkemeier.

Dondra and Gina have worked with me for several years as we integrated faith and neuroscience to help our clients align with God's created reality. We developed methods to help people understand how God designed our brains to function optimally. Their guidebook is an excellent example of how we help people develop and maintain optimal brain health and fitness.

God speaks to us through our brains. The Faithful Brain Model of Human Development is based on the idea that when our brains are guided by God, we are healthier, happier, and more resilient.

The exercises that Dondra and Gina have developed for this guidebook will help you understand the principles that I describe in *Your Faithful Brain: Designed for So Much More!* They have taken some of the more difficult topics and presented them in new ways that will help you apply the Faithful Brain Model to your life and the lives of your loved ones.

I know you're in for a wonderful experience as you settle in and enjoy what Dondra and Gina have prepared for you.

Leonard N. Matheson, PhD

OUR DEEPEST GRATITUDE

We (Dondra and Gina) want to thank Dr. Matheson for the opportunity to create this guidebook. We pray it enhances and expands your experience of *Your Faithful Brain: Designed for So Much More!* We are deeply indebted to our spouses and kids (Dondra's family: Brian, Darby, Sydney, and Aubrey. Gina's family: Tom, Sam, Ariel, Alex, Ben, and Alexander) for their patience and support throughout the creation of this book. We also thank the countless friends and colleagues who offered encouragement, an ear to bend, an eye to read, or a shoulder to cry on.

This book would not be what it is without the input of Ginger Moran, developmental editor extraordinaire, Melinda Martin, master of all things publishing and designing, and Shayla Eaton, a true guru of proofing and all things detail without whom we would've completely missed a lot of important pieces!

You have each been incredible to work with. We couldn't have done this without your guidance, hand-holding at times, and calm confidence that brought us out of the rafters when our uncertainty got the best of us.

Ultimately, we are filled with the most humble gratitude to our Savior Jesus Christ whose grace made it all possible and the leading of the Holy Spirit who provided the creativity and like-mindedness for us to make this project a reality.

As a result, we are forever changed and forever grateful.

In Grace,

Dondra & Gina

Contents

Introduction: Why the Heart-Brain Connection?...1

Start Here! (No, really. You're going to need this info!) 9

Chapter 1: A Faithful Brain Is Intentional 9

Chapter 2: A Faithful Brain Is Redemptive 29

Chapter 3: A Faithful Brain Is Integrative 45

Chapter 4: A Faithful Brain Is Relational 59

Chapter 5: A Faithful Brain Is Rehabilitative 75

Chapter 6: A Faithful Brain Is Truth-Guided 91

Chapter 7: A Faithful Brain Is Balanced 105

Chapter 8: A Faithful Brain Is Loving 115

Appendix A: Tips for Groups, Leaders & Facilitators 143

Appendix B: Definitions and Key Terms 147

Appendix C: Who Did We Quote? (More on additional authors) 151

Contact Info: We Want to Hear from You! 169

Introduction

WHY THE HEART-BRAIN CONNECTION?

Do not conform to the pattern of this world, but be transformed by the renewing of your mind. Then you will be able to test and approve what God's will is—His good, pleasing and perfect will.

—Romans 12:2 (NIV)
Apostle Paul (45 AD)

"The greatest discovery of my generation is that a human being can alter his life by altering his attitudes of mind."

—William James (1902)

Ever try to walk in two directions at the same time? Seems like a silly question, we are sure. This would require an impossible division of ourselves, each part heading in a different direction. We realize this is not only impossible but also undesirable. Yet, in many ways, this is exactly how we live.

We live *di-vi-ded*.

This division is the result of our discontent. Not the source of it, the *result*.

Can you feel it? See it?

We are dis-integrated—from God. Others. Our environment. From ourselves.

Are we reaching? You decide. We offer this for your consideration.

If we slow down and really pay attention, we find the whole of society breeds and teaches discontent—with what we have, how we look, what we believe. Who. We. Are.

This isn't new. Humanity has always been searching, hoping, looking. The discontent is palpable. Our world encourages us to obtain the external in order to satisfy the internal. The problem? It doesn't work that way. We don't work that way. When we try to make it work, we become divided. One from another, from ourselves, our environment.

From God.

Internally, we are disconnected—heart from mind, psyche from soul. We are a house divided. And we feel the weight of it. Discontent is heavy. Under it, we cannot stand.

Can you see it? Do *you* feel it?

The quest for more, better, beauty, power is evidenced everywhere we look. We don't even need to look that hard. The frenetic pace with which we pursue the "more" is exhausting and disorienting at best, depressing and debilitating at worst. And the results are evidenced in America's designation as the most medicated society on the planet. Research states that "nearly 13 prescriptions were prescribed per man, woman, and child last year . . Rx have slowly grown to be the third highest medical cost. *Welcome to the pill nation*" (Center for Research on Globalization, 2014; author's emphasis added).

While science is helping us realize the negative impact the quest for "more" is having on our lives and relationships, Scripture has always pointed us toward the consequences of living disconnected and discontented.

We see this first in the story of the Fall in Genesis. Once uncertainty and distrust entered the story, our story, they paved the way for pain, betrayal, brokenness, and a whole host of destructive thoughts, emotions, and behaviors. The impact was beyond spiritual. The entire makeup of man was impacted. We call this the *Science of the Fall*.

What do we mean by the Science of the Fall?

People tend to look at the Fall as a purely spiritual occurrence. We think there is more to it, and thinking in terms of only the spiritual implications limits our understanding of its full ramifications. As a result of the Fall, a literal dis-integration from God, others, and, consequently, ourselves occurred. Uncertainty and insecurity entered in, and we've been experiencing the impact ever since.

But how do we tie this to our brain's development and abilities? In Curt Thompson's book *Anatomy of the Soul,* he explores the idea that sin (choices that are not in line with how God has created us to live) is an issue of choosing to be mindless, which leads to our "minds becoming *dis-integrated*" (emphasis and hyphen added). Our brains are affected by the Fall as much as our souls are.

The Fall opened the door for brokenness on multiple levels. The dis-integration of key relationships (where uncertainty and distrust enter in) feeds negative pathways in our brain. This occurs in the brain and is played out in the body through our behaviors and emotions. When we rehearse these thoughts, they become embedded patterns and behaviors. It is the reality we operate from that impacts our overall well-being. Then we bring these behaviors into every situation and relationship in our lives.

This is what we believe is the Science of the Fall. It is the dis-ease that leads to the quest for "more."

But Scripture, as well as Science, also points us to solutions to our dis-ease. The idea that both Science and Faith point in the same direction regarding our dis-integrated lives and how we can best work to become more integrated was the motivation for Dr. Matheson to write *Your Faithful Brain: Designed for So Much More!* It's also why we felt compelled to write this guidebook based on his original text. We do not believe that Science and Faith are antithetical to one another. In fact, we believe the exact opposite to be true.

In the context of our overall health and wellness, the connection is clear. Over 2,800 studies have been done on the relationship between faith and wellness (*Handbook on Religion and Health*). Of those studies, an overwhelming 85 percent show engagement in faith practices had a positive effect on health and wellness while the other 15 percent of the studies show either no connection or a negative connection (**all of those included in that 15 percent viewed God as punitive and/or unsafe**).

We recognize a giant chasm has traditionally existed between Faith and Science. One could argue that, for the most part, Science has been seen as a "brain thing" while Faith has been identified as a "heart thing."

We make the case that both Science and Faith are a brain *and* heart thing. To appropriately explore either of these requires us to stop separating our brain and heart.

Scripture has always remained consistent in the message of how we are designed to optimally develop, yet Science continues to change and learn. Things once thought true have been disproved or modified. An often quoted example of this is found in Isaiah 40:22. Written around 587 BC, the author in Isaiah says about God that he is "enthroned above the circle of the earth." This idea—that the earth is round—was once dismissed as mere poetry and perhaps a nod toward the inaccuracy of the Bible because the belief was that the world was flat. Yet for centuries now, we have known that our world is, indeed, round.

For our purposes here in reflecting the ideas of Science and the brain, another example would be the widelyheld thought that humans are born with a finite number of brain cells and once those die, that's it. We now know that is not the case. Concepts like neuro-epigenesis (birth of neurons that happens throughout our lifetime) and neuroplasticity (the constant pruning and linking of neurons) help us understand that our brains are capable of growth throughout the life cycle. In fact, the Science of this truth is a core tenet of Dr. Matheson's book along with the Scripture that points to our ability to change our brains throughout life: "Be transformed by the renewing of your mind" (Romans 12:2, NIV). The tense of "renewing" implies a perpetual event: *always* renewing.

There was a time when the chasm between Faith and Science was the result of perceived inadequacies of Faith and its classification as unintelligent. But the more we learn in Science, the closer scientific knowledge moves to aspects of reality Faith has always been pointing toward. With each instance, the chasm becomes smaller.

Other concepts that reflect the alignment of Faith and Science are ones like the practice of gratitude. While one might say, "Yes, but all religions and spiritual practices prescribe the benefits of a gratitude practice," we humbly suggest that you consider these practices provide benefits not because they are all the same, but rather because our brains are *created* by a Creator who designed our brains to work best under the influence of such practices.

And if you're willing to consider this, would it not make sense to explore what else this Creator says about optimal development and how we see this affirmed in Science?

Then there is the vast amount of Scripture pertaining to the power of love, forgiveness, relationship, and connection. Through Science, we are learning more and more just how accurate these ideas are and how imperative love and relationship are if we hope to live longer, healthier lives.

This guidebook is designed to help you explore such ideas. We will address mind and emotional development through exercises involving various parts of the brain, explore their connection with the heart, and show you how Scripture speaks to each of these concepts.

We hope that through these chapters you will embrace a new way of thinking about the relationship between Faith and Science. The guidebook is based on Dr. Matheson's book and, while the exercises are based in specific chapters of it, we strongly encourage you to enhance the journey of deepening your understanding of how Faith and Science work together by reading Dr. Matheson's original book in its entirety. In it you will find a wealth of additional Science and Faith connections as well as his personal journey into living "life to the full."

Our deepest hope is that you will learn the importance of being intentional about developing the healthiest internal you possible and living this out in ways that improve your relationships with others, your world, yourself, and, ultimately, God.

Our desire is to help you discover how you can live life to the full every day, no matter what your circumstances may be. We believe you can live this beyond what you've ever experienced. Through our own personal journeys, education, and practice in the Faithful Brain Model, we have discovered that joy is a state of the soul rather than a state of circumstances. This joy leads to a full life lived out through an integrated self—a heart-brain connection, if you will.

And we are confident this is most wholly found at the intersection of Faith and Science.

START HERE

(No, really. You're going to need this info!)

Your guidebook is designed to take you deeper into the development of optimal brain health and fitness. You will find it is more than an overview of *Your Faithful Brain: Designed for So Much More!* (referred to as *YFB*). Because of that, the information below is critical to ensure that you can fully engage with the material to the best of your ability.

The *YFB* guidebook is an expansion on the material in the original text. There are quotes from other authors and sources to enhance your learning experience. While the original text lends itself to the understanding of the relationship between Faith and Science, the *YFB* guidebook seeks to bring the *YFB* material to a level of deeper connection with heart and soul.

> In the *YFB* guidebook, you will **NOT** be studying the original text of *Your Faithful Brain* in the order it was written. We have combined chapters of the original text in order to follow each theme of the *YFB* guidebook chapters.

Each chapter has been designed in a series of levels to deepen the interaction with the material from the original *Your Faithful Brain* book. Each level has exercises to improve your overall brain health and development. Although each can stand on its own, each level builds on the one before in this order: **ASSESS, ALIGN, ACCELERATE,** and **ACCEPT.** The title of each level gives you some insight into its goal.

ASSESS: In this level, you will ASSESS what you read in the original text. Through exploring how much you agree or disagree with key statements, ASSESS gives you insight into how much your thoughts and beliefs line up with those in the chapter.

ALIGN: This level will help you ALIGN with intentional brain development. "Just-Right Challenges" combine thought and action to give deeper significance to the material. Just-Right Challenges are those that demand the performance of a meaningful task that slightly exceeds your ability, harnessing neuroplasticity (making and breaking connections in the brain). HEADS UP: In some chapters, there will be an opportunity to participate in a DAILY activity. When you see this symbol at the beginning of a chapter, you will want to check for this DAILY activity.

ACCELERATE: This level will help you ACCELERATE your interaction with the original book by exploring your thoughts and feelings through a series of questions and exercises.

ACCEPT: In ACCEPT, you will have an opportunity to engage heart, mind, and soul with additional material inspired by the chapter. Although designed as the final level, you may want to read it earlier in order to prime your understanding of the concepts discussed.

At the end of this guidebook, you will find additional information to help guide you through the exercises and reading. We've expanded on important and often repeated terms that are found in this guidebook and in the original *YFB* book. Should you decide to experience this book with a few friends or take it into a group setting, you will find helpful hints and ideas at the end.

We've also provided you with a brief sketch of the authors we've quoted throughout this book to give you ways to further your journey.

1

DAILY

A faithful brain is
INTENTIONAL

Therefore, I urge you, brothers and sisters, in view of God's mercy, to offer your bodies as a living sacrifice, holy and pleasing to God—this is your true and proper worship. Do not conform to the pattern of this world, but be transformed by the renewing of your mind. Then you will be able to test and approve what God's will is—his good, pleasing and perfect will.

—Romans 12:1–2 (NIV)

"The kind of truth that makes us free is when our minds and our hearts begin to agree with God and we begin to see things the way He does. It remakes us. It transforms us."

—Bob Hamp

We begin the *Your Faithful Brain... Ignited!* guidebook by exploring "A Faithful Brain Is Intentional," Chapter 11 of *YFB*. Why do we start with the last chapter of the *YFB* book? Because without intention, developing a faithful brain becomes impossible.

Developing what Dr. Matheson refers to as a faithful brain doesn't happen by accident. It requires intentional thought and action like goal-setting, participating in communities of faith, and the exercises presented here.

Although intention isn't enough, it's necessary. Without the intention to develop a faithful brain, you won't get anywhere. Intention, applied properly, helps you align your brain with God's created reality (how He has designed you, others, and the world to work best) as you learn that "you were designed for so much more!"

The beauty is that in terms of "more," you, along with God, get to intentionally decide *what* "more" is for you.

(P.S. If you skipped it, now is a good time to go back and read the "START HERE" portion of this book. It will only take a few minutes but will significantly enhance how you use this guidebook. If you have already read it, good for you! Journey on!)

▶ **Read Chapter 11 of *YFB: A Faithful Brain Is Intentional.***

ASSESS

Circle the number that best describes your thoughts, opinions, and feelings about each statement.

1 – – – – –2– – – – –3– – – – – 4– – – – –5– – – – – 6

| Disagree | Disagree | Disagree | Agree | Agree | Agree |
| Completely | Somewhat | Slightly | Slightly | Somewhat | Completely |

1. **As it says in Romans 12:1–2, it is important to be intentional about renewing my mind.**

    1 – – – – –2– – – – –3– – – – – 4– – – – –5– – – – – 6

2. **Joy is my brain's "designed" response when I'm closer to God than to my circumstances.**

    1 – – – – –2– – – – –3– – – – – 4– – – – –5– – – – – 6

3. **Intentional development of my brain starts by adopting the character of Jesus.**

    1 – – – – –2– – – – –3– – – – – 4– – – – –5– – – – – 6

4. **God is completely dependable.**

1— — — — —2— — — — —3— — — — —4— — — — —5— — — — —6

5. **Joy starts with making a choice to allow God's presence to impact me more than my circumstances.**

1— — — — —2— — — — —3— — — — —4— — — — —5— — — — —6

6. **I cannot develop a faithful brain in isolation.**

1— — — — —2— — — — —3— — — — —4— — — — —5— — — — —6

7. **I can see a connection between surrendering to God and experiencing serenity.**

1— — — — —2— — — — —3— — — — —4— — — — —5— — — — —6

8. **Regarding the last seven questions, I can see a connection between experiencing serenity and joy.**

1— — — — —2— — — — —3— — — — —4— — — — —5— — — — —6

Write out the statement you **agree** with most. _____

_____

_____

Why do you agree with this particular statement more than the others?

_____

_____

_____

_____

Write out the statement you **disagree** with most. _____

_____

_____

Why do you disagree with this particular statement more than the others?

_____

_____

_____

_____

ALIGN I

> "Only in relationship with the other am I free."
>
> —Dietrich Bonhoeffer

In this first Align section, you are given the opportunity to set the intention of this study. It begins by exploring where you are in life now and where you want to be.

PART A

Dr. Matheson asks, "What's one thing that would make life more worth living?" While you may have several answers to this question, our goal is to set an intention for this study. In light of that goal, what is one answer you would give to that question? Write it out here.

_____

_____

_____

_____

_____

_____

_____

PART B

What are the steps necessary to make this happen?

_____
_____
_____
_____
_____

PART C

Identify one or two people with whom you will share this information and give them a copy in writing. Ask them to pray for and with you and invite them to hold you accountable for taking the steps necessary to achieve your goal.

Write their names here:

_____
_____
_____

ALIGN II

Another important theme of Chapter 11 in the original text of *YFB* is joy. Joy isn't the same thing as happiness. While happiness depends on what "happens," joy is something we can set an intention to have even in the midst of difficult circumstances.

Having joy begins by recognizing its origin is in our closeness to God. Sometimes our dependence on our circumstances stands in the way of us receiving and experiencing the joy God has set before us.

By joy, we mean something more than mere happiness. An important component of optimal brain health is recognizing our ability to hold more than one emotion in tension at one time; for example, allowing ourselves to experience both joy and sorrow at the same time.

A recent example of holding emotions in tension from my (Gina's) life was our family reunion this year. We laughed till our cheeks burned from smiling and loved till our arms were tired from hugging. And right in the middle of it all was a memorial for my cousin Cheryl and my uncle Dick who are no longer with us. Remembering brought sorrow and at the same time enhanced our joy, recalling their love for family and the special place we hold our reunion. It also increased our level of connection.

This concept of holding emotions in tension rather than attempting to numb or dull emotions like sadness is important. Denying our reality when it's painful leads to a whole host of problems. One that might shock you is that it leads to a numbing or dulling of our joy.

Why? Because we can't selectively numb our emotions. If we numb the grief or pain, we numb our joy.

With God, we have the capability to experience some level of joy in even the most difficult circumstances.

Start each day by asking God to help you see the joy He places in your life. At the end of each day or the next morning, reflect and write what He revealed to you.

Essentially, what we're asking you to do is engage in a practice of gratitude. This exercise will reach its fullest impact if you practice it for at least thirty days. We know this is true because it aligns with what we know about birth, maturation, and linkage of neurons. It takes around thirty days for this process to happen (which is why we need to practice something for at least thirty days before it becomes a habit).

This is also an important step in developing a habit of intentionality. Being grateful won't just happen. You will need to focus and decide to be grateful. If we can be intentional about finding things to be grateful for, it helps us build intention in other areas of our lives.

> "You will show me the way of life, granting me the joy of your presence and the pleasures of living with you forever."
>
> —Psalm 16:11 (NLT)

Gratitude is one of the most fundamental tools to helping us improve our brain's integration along with proven efficacy in the fight against things like depression, anxiety, and negative thinking.

What we find of further interest is that all spiritual practices around the globe—regardless of what they are, even for those who don't subscribe to a particular god or set of beliefs—have a practice of gratitude as one of their core tenets. This is not because just any type of spirituality will work, but rather because we've been created by the God of the universe to have our brains work best under the influence of a practice of gratitude.

But here's a bit of caution. While you are beginning to explore a gratitude practice, it is perfectly normal to focus on things that are circumstantial or material. What we would like you to work on is expanding your joyfulness. There are a few reasons for this. First and foremost, it is important to practice reflecting on things that bring us joy and that we can be grateful for that have nothing to do with circumstances or material things. We want our ability to be grateful and our truest state of joy to come from God and how He shows Himself to us through our relationships.

Another important reason to reflect on relationships is because it provides more of a whole-brain experience, allowing many parts of our brain to work together to call up an image of someone (for instance, "Thank you, God, for my son's smile at just the right moment today.") and reflect on the emotions tied to that relationship. This is particularly beneficial when reflecting at the end of the day before bed. It can set a sense of calm in us and help us rest better.

Finally, as we develop our lens of gratitude, we will begin to operate out of a place of joyfulness. This is a deeper state of joy than mere happiness, which almost always depends on circumstances. When our joy is more of an *it is well with my soul* state of being as described in the story coming up in the next section, it manifests in how we do life with those around us.

Here are a few spaces to get you started on this practice. We recommend getting a journal specifically for gratitude practices and keeping it near your bedside. Perhaps an additional piece that you may find beneficial is to write a bit about how you feel you are doing in areas of gratitude and living out that gratitude in your daily life. How is your emotional state at present? Take an inventory and, at the end of thirty days, take another one. See what changes you have experienced as a result of this practice.

Day 1: _____

_____

_____

_____

Day 2: _____

_____

_____

_____

Day 3: _____

_____

_____

_____

Day 4: _____

_____

_____

_____

Day 5: _____

_____

_____

_____

➡ ACCELERATE I

Before we enter into the important questions that help us reflect on intentionality and joy, let's look at a story that might give us a clearer idea of the deeper meaning of joy.

The year was 1873. A prosperous lawyer by the name of Horatio Spafford was living in Chicago with his young wife Anna, age twenty-seven, and their four daughters, eleven-year-old Anna (Annie), nine-year-old Margaret Lee (Maggie), five-year-old Elizabeth (Bessie), and two-year-old Tanetta. It had been a rough couple of years for the Spafford family, first losing their son to illness, then enduring the Chicago Fire and, shortly after, Anna becoming ill, likely due to loss and stress. Horatio decided it would benefit the family, and especially his wife's health, to join friends on an extended vacation in Europe.

But when the time approached for departure, Horatio was unexpectedly detained in Chicago on business. Not wanting to further disappoint his family, he sent Anna and their daughters on ahead so they could start their vacation. They boarded the *SS Ville du Havre* with excitement and anticipation of a much-needed holiday. Undoubtedly, the children chattered on about what adventures they would have on board ship and abroad in Europe. Anna, undoubtedly, hoped for much needed respite.

Alas, adventure and respite were not to be. On the evening of November 11, 1873, the *SS Ville du Havre* was rammed midship by the *Loch Earn*, a British iron sailing ship. The *SS Ville du Havre* sunk in twelve minutes in waters three miles deep. Anna was found unconscious, floating on a piece of debris, but Annie, Maggie, Bessie, and Tanetta were lost at sea.

Several days later, Horatio received a telegram from Anna that read, "Saved alone. What shall I do?"

Undoubtedly heartbroken, Horatio left Chicago immediately to get Anna and bring her home. On the ship crossing the Atlantic headed toward home, the captain called Horatio to his cabin to tell him they were about to pass over the spot where his four daughters were lost in waters three miles deep. He would later write to his sister-in-law, Rachel, "On last Thursday, we passed over the spot where she went down. Three miles deep. But I do not think of our dear ones there. They are safe, folded, the dear lambs."

And it was there that Horatio found himself penning these words as he passed over their watery grave:

> *When peace like a river attendeth my way,*
> *when sorrows like sea billows roll*
> *Whatever my lot, thou hast taught me to say,*
> **It is well, it is well, with my soul**

He wrote these powerful words, not in the midst of a celebration or success, but in the eye of a storm of grief. Horatio knew what we all too often forget: happiness, in the common, traditional sense, is predicated on circumstances and is a situational state. There is something deeper that can't be taken away based on circumstances.

Joy, the *it is well with my soul* joy, is a state of our soul predicated on our proximity to God. This is one of the most challenging yet important concepts to grasp. We can hang on to joy, not the "joy, joy, joy down in my heart" of a Sunday school song, but soul-grounding joy, regardless of what is happening in our lives, not to the exclusion of grieving or struggling but along with it. Oh, how our lives would be, could be changed if we not only understood this, but also lived it out.

This is more than a spiritual perspective. It is imperative to grasp this. Horatio understood what science is helping us understand. The first step in finding our joy is to accept our reality as it truly is, not as we wish it would be.

Psychiatrist and author, David Viscott, states in his book *Emotional Resilience,* "Healing begins when we can let go of the hope that things are different than they really are."

This is a challenging thought! Consciously, we think that if we accept our reality, we are somehow agreeing with it or saying it's okay. Subconsciously, we believe that by refusing to accept things as they really are, we can somehow change our circumstances or, at a minimum, diminish their impact. When pointed out, we see this is irrational. But when left to our inner dialogue, we do not recognize this exercise in futility.

Denying our reality when it's painful leads to a whole host of problems. First and foremost, you may be surprised to know that it leads to a numbing or dulling of our joy. Why? Because, as we said earlier, we can't selectively numb our emotions. If we numb the grief and pain, we numb the joy.

You may be asking how this can be possible. All emotions are initiated and managed in the same portion of the brain: the limbic system. The limbic system is a complex set of brain structures composed of the hypothalamus, hippocampus, amygdala, and other structures that link the brain stem with the cerebral cortex. If we practice disconnection from this region of the brain, we disconnect from all of the emotions.

Science has also shown us that denying our pain leads to depression, unhealthy and addictive behaviors, and disconnection. (Yes, from others, God, and self. Are you picking up on the theme here?) Practicing acceptance of reality leaves room for us to choose joy.

What is your definition of "it is well with my soul"?_____

_____

_____

_____

_____

ACCELERATE II

> "JOY IS OUR BRAIN'S NATURAL RESPONSE WHEN WE'RE CLOSER TO GOD THAN WE ARE TO OUR CIRCUMSTANCES."
>
> —Len Matheson

1. Read Kay Warren's words on pages 183–184 in the *How Can I Find Joy in Difficult Circumstances?* section of the *YFB* book. How is your belief about joy impacted by her perspective?

   _____
   _____
   _____
   _____

2. In Chapter 11's section, *How Did Danny Teach You about Joy?*, what does the statement "meaningful goals can be brain-protective" mean to you?

   _____
   _____
   _____
   _____

3. What does "living intentionally" (page 191) mean to you?

4. In what ways can you relate to Paul in Romans 7:15–19 as described on page 178?

5. Name the most recent time that your circumstances robbed you of your joy.

6. What kind of feelings come up for you when you read the statement "God is completely dependable; people are not" on page 186 in section *Why Was Danny's Dependence on God Important?*

7. Have you made a decision to choose joy? If yes, how did you come to that decision? If not, what is preventing you from being able to choose joy?

_____

_____

_____

8. What is your biggest takeaway from Chapter 11 of *YFB*? How will you use it to impact your life today?

_____

_____

_____

_____

"Let's not be afraid to receive each day's surprise, whether it comes as sorrow or joy. It will open a new place in our hearts."

—Henri Nouwen

ACCEPT

> "AND HOPE DOES NOT PUT US TO SHAME, BECAUSE GOD'S LOVE HAS BEEN POURED OUT INTO OUR HEARTS THROUGH THE HOLY SPIRIT, WHO HAS BEEN GIVEN TO US."
>
> —Romans 5:5 (ESV)

Although Chapter 11 is chronologically the conclusion of our journey through *Your Faithful Brain*, it holds some of the most important, foundational clues to working through this guidebook in ways that bring us closer to God. And it does this in a way that brings us joy and hope instead of shame and discouragement.

As people who have accepted Jesus Christ as Savior, we take great comfort in reading the words of Paul, who sometimes struggled with doing the right thing at the right time (Romans 7:15–19). We can all relate to this.

But it is also encouraging to read the words in Hebrews 4:15 (NIV): "For we do not have a high priest who is unable to empathize with our weaknesses, but we have one who has been tempted in every way, just as we are—yet he did not sin." So, when it comes to our mistakes, that means God understands our struggles, especially when our circumstances get the best of us.

But what does *that* mean?

Before we answer that question, there are a few others we may need to address first.

Have you come to believe that your circumstances do not dictate your level of joy? Notice, we did not say "happiness." We said "joy."

That may be hard to answer, especially when our circumstances are "difficult at best."

What we are really asking is, have you come to trust God enough in all your circumstances to have your best interests at heart (Jeremiah 29:11)?

You see, if you have not reached that place in your faith journey yet, the rest of what you are being asked to consider here may leave you frustrated and a bit undone. We would encourage you to first take care of any business you need to address with God—anger, hurt, distrust, fear, shame, doubt. He already knows it anyway. The addressing is more for you than for Him. And if you find this a struggle, this may be a journey best shared with a professional counselor or spiritual mentor to help you understand the places where you feel stuck or unsure.

And because each of us is at a different place in our faith, you may need to start with a simple prayer asking God to show you He is real and so is His grace and mercy. (We said simple, not easy.)

You may be thinking to yourself, "Okay, but I've already done all of that. What is my next step?"

We're glad you asked! Your next step is deeper. It involves recognizing that, because God gets that we mess up, He already took care of it. He found a way to keep us connected to Him throughout our struggles through His Son, Jesus. So, our responsibility (outside of accepting that free gift of salvation) is to live *intentionally*, cultivating that connection through *developing our character to be more like Christ* and to work through our struggles with authenticity and transparency.

Dr. Matheson tells us that he uses the image of himself as a child in order to remind him of his capacity for joy. We hope you will find a picture of yourself as well that reminds you of your capacity for joy.

By the way, did you know that Jesus has an image of joy too? Hebrews 12:2 (ESV) tells us that Jesus "endured the cross for the joy set before Him."

While part of that joy is to be with the Father in heaven, guess what the other part of that joy is?

All of us! It is all of us who have accepted the gift of Christ and call Jesus our Lord and Savior—all of us who could not save ourselves.

No matter what mistakes we have made (or continue to make), Jesus loved us enough to endure the cross on our behalf. Does that beautifully wreck you like it does me? If so, then let that deep love wash over you.

And remember that in Romans 8:1, we are told "there is no condemnation for those who are in Christ Jesus." Allow that to be your constant reminder that He has enough grace for your journey.

Let Jesus be our example to choose joy in all of our circumstances. Let us allow the hope of Jesus, as we become more like Him, to guide us through our circumstances. Let us allow Jesus to guide us through this life so that we may choose joy in every circumstance.

And, since joy is contagious, let's start an epidemic!

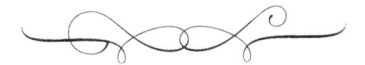

"We are created for joy. Not a weak and watery concept of joy that merely dilutes our sadness and pain. Rather, it is the hard deck on which all of life finds its legs; a byproduct of deeply connected relationships in which each member is consummately known."

—*The Soul of Shame*, Curt Thompson

2

A faithful brain is
REDEMPTIVE

"God creates out of nothing. Wonderful you say. Yes, to be sure, but he does what is still more wonderful: he makes saints out of sinners."

—Søren Kierkegaard

But because of his great love for us, God, who is rich in mercy, made us alive with Christ even when we were dead in transgressions—it is by grace you have been saved.

—Ephesians 2:4–5 (NIV)

While the concept of redemption is seen throughout *YFB*, it is the central focus of Chapter 1. In seeking optimal brain health, most of us recognize that our brains have been damaged. This damage can come in a variety of ways from relational, emotional challenges to actual physical brain injury; all of which can cause our brains to operate in dysfunctional ways.

Our growing relationship with God enables our brains to experience a deeper level of restoration or redemption to our optimal brain health. In this chapter, we will explore how redemption is key to the development of optimal brain health and to finding our place in God's created reality (how He has designed you, others, and the world to work best).

▶ **Read *Your Brain Is Designed for Redemption and Rehabilitation*, Chapter 1 of *YFB*.**

ASSESS

"No matter how old you are and no matter what you've done or what's been done to you, your brain can ALWAYS be rehabilitated. It's never too late for redemption and rehabilitation."

—Len Matheson

Circle the number that best describes your thoughts, opinions, and feelings about each statement.

1 — — — —2— — — — —3— — — — — 4— — — —5— — — — 6

| Disagree | Disagree | Disagree | Agree | Agree | Agree |
| Completely | Somewhat | Slightly | Slightly | Somewhat | Completely |

1. **I feel like I am "living life to the full" the way Jesus describes in John 10:10.**

   1 — — — —2— — — — —3— — — — 4— — — —5— — — — 6

2. **I can see how the choices I have made have impacted my brain's development.**

   1 — — — —2— — — — —3— — — — 4— — — —5— — — — 6

3. *Actively* engaging in God's created reality is vitally important to developing a faithful brain.

   1- - - - -2- - - - -3- - - - - 4- - - - -5- - - - - 6

4. Trusting God and following Jesus's example optimizes brain growth.

   1- - - - -2- - - - -3- - - - - 4- - - - -5- - - - - 6

5. I trust Jesus completely for redemption.

   1- - - - -2- - - - -3- - - - - 4- - - - -5- - - - - 6

6. I want to cocreate my life with God.

   1- - - - -2- - - - -3- - - - - 4- - - - -5- - - - - 6

7. I believe it is never too late for redemption and rehabilitation, even for me.

   1- - - - -2- - - - -3- - - - - 4- - - - -5- - - - - 6

Write out the statement you **agree** with most. _____

_____

_____

Why do you agree with this particular statement more than the others?

_____

_____

_____

_____

Write out the statement you **disagree** with most. _____

_____

_____

Why do you disagree with that particular statement more than the others?

_____

_____

_____

_____

"God wants you to do your best and He'll do the rest."
—Father Robert Gipson

ALIGN

In this chapter, we emphasize the importance of aligning all facets of our being with God's created reality (how He has designed you, others, and the world to work best). Redemption or recovery of our brain health develops as we align with God's created reality, His will. An important part of this process is to examine where you are starting from.

PART A

We strongly encourage you to take the **Faithful Brain Fitness Challenge** and obtain your unique, customized Character Strengths Report (faithfulbrain.com/faithful-brain-fitness-assessment). It will be a valuable resource for other exercises through this guidebook. You can use the report in subsequent chapters for other FB challenges.

PART B

Rate how you feel each of these areas **aligns** with God's plan and purposes for your life:

$$1-----2-----3-----4$$

Completely out of Alignment   *Somewhat out of Alignment*   *Mostly Aligned*   *Completely Aligned*

1. **Physical: my physical health in general, exercise, sleep, nutrition, regular checkups**

    $$1-----2-----3-----4$$

2. **Mental: my emotional health, thoughts, feelings, judgments, observations**

    $$1-----2-----3-----4$$

3. **Spiritual: my vertical integration with God, integrity, prayer life, Bible study**

    $$1-----2-----3-----4$$

4. **Social:** my horizontal relationships with friends, coworkers, community

   1— — — — —2— — — — —3— — — — —4

5. **Financial:** my money matters, saving, giving, budgeting, preparedness

   1— — — — —2— — — — —3— — — — —4

6. **Family:** interactions with my family and extended family

   1— — — — —2— — — — —3— — — — —4

7. **Career:** my work activities, responsibilities, satisfaction, hopes, dreams

   1— — — — —2— — — — —3— — — — —4

In the first column, list the top three areas of your life (based on the above list) that are most important to you. In the second column, write a brief statement for each describing one way you could better align that area with God's plans and purposes for your life.

We started the list off with some examples.

Family	Set aside one night a week to spend focused time with my family
Spiritual	Start a Bible reading plan
Career	Be honest with coworkers when asked for input or when having difficulties

Which area will you start working on today?

_____

_____

What will you do in that area? _____

_____

_____

_____

Developing a Faithful Brain begins with paying attention. Paying attention requires intentionality. In other words, we need to pay attention to what we are paying attention to. Our minds are prone to wander. Yet every day, God is offering us opportunities to *wonder* about the things He sets before us.

Start your day by asking God to help you pay attention to His created reality (how He has designed you, others, and the world to work best).

Write down *one* thing each day that you notice or learn about God's reality for you:

Day 1: _____

_____

Day 2: _____

_____

Day 3: _____

_____

Day 4: _____

_____

Day 5: _____

_____

Day 6: _____

_____

Day 7: _____

_____

> "Hope protects the brain and heart and the rest of the nervous system so that neurorehabilitation (brain healing and growth) can unfold."
>
> —Len Matheson

➡ ACCELERATE

"WHAT GIVES ME THE MOST HOPE EVERY DAY IS GOD'S GRACE; KNOWING THAT HIS GRACE IS GOING TO GIVE ME THE STRENGTH FOR WHATEVER I FACE, KNOWING THAT NOTHING IS A SURPRISE TO GOD."

—Rick Warren

1. What do you think about the notion that it is never too late for redemption and rehabilitation? Can you see how hope connects with this idea?

   _____
   _____
   _____

2. Given the perspective offered in the quote on page 7 that says, "Hope protects the brain and heart and the rest of the nervous system so that neurorehabilitation can unfold." What are some of the ways that you have experienced God's protective hope in your own life? This does not necessarily mean a time when everything worked out the way you wanted it to. Perhaps it's a memory of a time when, despite the circumstances, you later recognized that God provided His protective hope for you. Perhaps in reading this, you're realizing for the first time there was an instance when God Himself provided that hope.

   _____
   _____
   _____

3. What did you think about the story of Peter (pages 2–5)? Were you surprised by his changes? What hope did you receive from his story?

_____
_____
_____

4. What do you think about the idea that your choices impact your brain's development?

_____
_____
_____

5. Can you guess at how some of the choices you've made have possibly limited your brain growth? List them here.

_____
_____
_____

6. Can you imagine how God might work to redeem a choice you wish you had not made and its consequences? Write about the redemption you have seen. Also, write a few ways God could still be working out His redemptive purposes or in what ways you hope He will work out His redemptive purposes.

_____
_____
_____
_____

7. Name the hope God is offering you at this time.

   _____

   _____

   _____

8. If you are struggling to name the hope, ask God to show you an area that you feel is beyond hope, and let Him show you what hope might look like in that situation. Remembering that hope is not always fulfilled by everything working out the way we want. Write your thoughts here.

   _____

   _____

   _____

   _____

9. What is your biggest takeaway from Chapter 1 of *YFB*? How will you use it to impact your life today?

   _____

   _____

   _____

   _____

✝ ACCEPT

John 10:10 (NIV) says, "The thief comes only to steal and kill and destroy; I have come that they may have life, and have it to the full."

The book, *Your Faithful Brain: Designed for So Much More!*, and this guidebook can help you explore how God created you (and your brain) so you can live life to the full. And we believe a redeemed life is a full life.

Are you enjoying your life? This thought-provoking question needs to be answered honestly. Your truthfulness says a great deal about you, which is all that matters. Only when you acknowledge your vulnerability can you begin to recognize there is something or Someone greater than you. Life is full of all kinds of moments. Not all are enjoyable. However, it is possible to make the best of every moment, and, in doing so, we experience a fuller life. Are you willing to admit you are not experiencing all that you would like to be? A person's ego can sometimes keep them from doing what is best for them. Sometimes, it is more about a struggle or false belief that is holding you back. Maybe there is an underlying issue that needs addressing, something that is not meant to be gone through alone.

It is possible to experience a fuller life because there is a Resource that has been acknowledged since the beginning of time. God exists! God is the "Someone," the One who is there for you and everyone else, no matter what; all it takes is a willingness on your part to surrender to the "Someone" greater than you. We know that is often more difficult than we just made it sound. But it is, nonetheless, true.

John 10:10 says, "The thief comes only to steal and kill and destroy; I have come that they may have life, and have it to the full." The full passage of Scripture from which this verse is taken describes Jesus as a shepherd. The verses before and after John 10:10 explain how shepherds protect their sheep and the sheep trust their shepherd. Jesus is the Good Shepherd, but the contrast described in this verse provides an image, the thief, coming to make your life less enjoyable and, in some cases, to completely destroy it. This is the opposite of Jesus's promise, which is a life that is full if you follow His lead.

So, what does it mean to "have life to the full?" It means to have life as God intended, not necessarily what we intended. To be focused less on the circumstances of this life and more on what we are created for. The more you are "in sync" with God's created reality, how He designed us to operate in relationship with Him, with others, and with the community at large, the more we will experience "life to the full." This is not an abdication of responsibility or choice. Rather, this is a *concentrated effort to co-author our life* under God's direction. It is not an unrealistic promise of a problem-free life, but rather, an ability to experience a full life even in the midst of struggles.

God gave Jesus to you and everyone else. He gave us Jesus as an example of living life to the full. Jesus gave of Himself to demonstrate that a full life is comprised of integrity, commitment, willingness, obedience, surrender to God's will, and so much more. It is a mental, emotional, physical, and spiritual endeavor. Each one impacts the other.

The Holy Spirit is in you and everyone else who acknowledges their dependence on God. When that happens, although not everyone would say they "feel" different, at least not right away, the fact is a change has taken place within us. This needs to be explored and discovered. However, few would say life to the full is what they thought it would be. Yet the new experience is far greater than a life totally dependent upon the self. Experiencing life to the fullest is a process of growing in a relationship with God and learning to embrace the life He has designed. As we surrender the parts of our lives to His plans, our plans begin to align with His. We are able to enjoy life more fully, no matter what it might hold. Our obedience to the call God places on our lives takes us beyond the life we could have imagined for ourselves. When we read John 10:10 and the next few verses, Jesus says that He is "the good shepherd and that the good shepherd lays down His life for the sheep." The Shepherd stays with His sheep, helping them along the way. It is a picture of a life fully lived, albeit, not as we may have intended or envisioned. Jesus provides what is needed for each day. Sheep recognize being cared for and rest in that recognition.

This is important because as we move through life, challenges come our way. Our brain is designed to respond to challenges by growing. However, if the challenge is too demanding or if it comes along at a time in life that is already stressful due to other demands, stress chemicals like cortisol can persist at such a high level that the neuroplasticity (the brain's ability to re-organize itself by forming new neural connections) to support brain growth is diminished.

Being able to rest in the recognition of God's safety helps to minimize these stress chemicals so that challenges are more likely to produce growth. It creates an atmosphere conducive to growth rather than impairment.

Will we lose our way? Will we panic and strike out on our own? It is possible. Even in those moments, Jesus is still the Shepherd and through His Holy Spirit will pursue us and bring us back to Himself. He will also put others in our lives as examples and through community will help us train our faithful brains.

Trust God to take you where you need to go. Pray for His guidance as you engage with this material. Ask for Him to help you see His design for your life as one fully redeemed. Journal your initial thoughts and feelings about this process.

"We must free ourselves of the hope that the sea will ever rest. We must learn to sail in high winds."

Aristotle Onassis

3 DAILY

A faithful brain is
INTEGRATIVE

"Enlightenment is not about cocooning one's self but about integrating more fully with both yourself and life."
—Jay Goodwin

Love the Lord your God with all your heart, all your being, and all your strength.
—Deuteronomy 6:5 (CEB)

Chapters 2 and 3 of *YFB* are an exciting adventure into a deeper understanding of how neuroscience supports the Bible's integrated approach. A brain that is fully integrated with God, within itself, and with others allows us to realize the optimal design of our brain that God intended. For each of us as individuals, relational beings, and children of God, we can find a deeper grasp of what it means to love God with all our hearts, souls, and minds.

▶ **Read *The Faithful Brain of Jesus* (Chapter 2) and *A Faithful Brain Is God-Integrated* (Chapter 3) of *YFB*.**

⧗ ASSESS

Circle the number that best describes your thoughts, opinions, and feelings about each statement.

1 – – – – –2– – – – –3– – – – – 4– – – – –5– – – – – 6

Disagree Completely   *Disagree Somewhat*   *Disagree Slightly*   *Agree Slightly*   *Agree Somewhat*   *Agree Completely*

1. **I am challenging myself in ways that help develop my brain's capacity.**

    1 – – – – –2– – – – –3– – – – – 4– – – – –5– – – – – 6

2. **My relationship with Jesus is changing my brain.**

    1 – – – – –2– – – – –3– – – – – 4– – – – –5– – – – – 6

3. **Sin interferes with the integration of my heart, mind, and soul.**

    1 – – – – –2– – – – –3– – – – – 4– – – – –5– – – – – 6

4. **God is completely trustworthy.**

   1- - - - -2- - - - -3- - - - - 4- - - - -5- - - - - 6

5. **The root of emotional troubles and relational strife stems from a dis-integrated brain.**

   1- - - - -2- - - - -3- - - - - 4- - - - -5- - - - - 6

6. **Integration begins with God.**

   1- - - - -2- - - - -3- - - - - 4- - - - -5- - - - - 6

7. **I am intentional about my character development.**

   1- - - - -2- - - - -3- - - - - 4- - - - -5- - - - - 6

Write out the statement you **agree** with most. _____

Why do you agree with this particular statement more than the others?

Write out the statement you **disagree** with most. _____

Why do you disagree with that particular statement more than the others?

= ALIGN

> "God's love is the most powerful antidote to self-destructive hippocampal rehearsal."
>
> —Len Matheson

In this section, you have an opportunity to engage in constructive hippocampal rehearsal (see Carol's story, pages 45–48). When we practice recalling positive experiences, we are assisting God in creating a deeper integration between the creative, emotional, logical, decision-making areas of our brain. Even our senses of smell and sight get into the game. From a more scientific perspective, we are integrating the hippocampus and amygdala with other areas like the prefrontal cortex. Better communication and connection are created when we integrate these areas of the brain.

This is played out in how we communicate with others and interact with the world around us. What we believe, the decisions we make, and the way we respond to our life overall is significantly impacted by the health and level of integration of our minds and hearts. In short, this is called our character.

We can be intentional with regard to our character development by utilizing purposeful hippocampal rehearsal. While hippocampal rehearsal is an automatic process that is constantly creating, recreating, and reinforcing memories, we can be intentional in this rehearsal process as well. We can use our intentionality to influence our hippocampal rehearsal and enhance our character development to become more like Jesus.

Here's what we mean. Memories are consolidated as we sleep. The hippocampus plays a big role in this. In fact, those who are engaging in counseling with a Faithful Brain Counselor refer to this exercise as the Healthy Hippocampus Exercise.

By selecting what we think about as we drift off to sleep, we can direct the improvement of our self-narrative, which is developed largely through hippocampal rehearsal. I (Gina) often tell my clients, "The story you tell yourself most often is the one that becomes most true." We can be intentional about what that story is.

You may already be aware of a character strength that God is asking you to work on developing. If that's the case, simply choose it from the chart on page 58. But, if you are uncertain about what area you need/want to work on, we strongly encourage you to take the Faithful Brain Fitness Challenge and obtain your unique, customized report. Go to faithfulbrain.com/faithful-brain-fitness-assessment. Your report will be emailed to you. Once you receive your report, choose one character strength that you believe God is leading you to strengthen in your life.

Remember each character strength associates with a type of brain integration as discussed in Chapter 3 of the original text. The chart on page 58 is a reminder of how the character strengths relate to brain integration.

Brain Integration	Character Strength
Vertical	Hope
	Appreciation
	Gratitude
	Humor
	Humility
	Mercy
	Self-Control
	Prudence
	Vitality
	Dependability
	Bravery
	Persistence
Horizontal	Curiosity
	Open-mindedness
	Love of Learning
	Perspective
	Creativity
Social	Love of Learning
	Kindness
	Social Intelligence
	Citizenship
	Fairness
	Leadership

Daily Challenge:

Be deliberate about doing three things during your day that demonstrates your chosen character strength. For instance, with **Gratitude**:

1) Thanked my daughter for doing the dishes that night.

2) Wrote a quick note to a friend expressing my gratitude for her listening to me about my job situation.

3) Thanked God for His goodness to me in helping me with work dilemma.

Jot down a brief description (like above) of the three demonstrations of your chosen strength. Before going to sleep each night, prayerfully review with God these three episodes from the day. Keep reminding yourself of them until you fall asleep. This is the consolidation aspect of our practice. By focusing on those events in the day where we were able to engage and practice that character strength we are working to build, it becomes a stronger, more dominant part of our narrative. It becomes "more true" of us. By doing this, it also creates a greater likelihood that we will begin to act out of that strength in the future.

Do this every day for a week. Write down your three demonstrations of your character strength here.

Character Strength: _____

Day 1: _____

_____

_____

Day 2: _____

_____

_____

Day 3: _____

_____

_____

Day 4: _____

_____

_____

Day 5: _____

_____

_____

Day 6: _____

_____

_____

Day 7: _____

_____

_____

For optimal brain development, practice this exercise for thirty days. After thirty days, you may choose to repeat the exercise with a new character strength or continue with the same one if you feel it needs more strengthening.

➡ ACCELERATE

1. On page 19 of *Your Faithful Brain (YFB)*, there is a quote that says, "Behavior affects brain development and brain development affects behavior." How have you experienced this in your own life?

   _____

   _____

   _____

2. There are some important technical terms in Chapter 2. Define each term in your own words. Which one stands out to you the most and why?

   Neural networks: _____

   _____

   Neuroplasticity: _____

   _____

   Neurogenesis: _____

   _____

   Neural epigenesis: _____

   _____

3. In the space below, create two lists. In the first column, write some ways you have protected or developed your brain. In column two, write some ways you have not protected or developed your brain.

Brain Protective	Non-Protective

4. On page 25 of *Your Faithful Brain*, it says, "Jesus changed His disciples' brains by offering new life within the context of God's trustworthy love." What are some ways you have experienced God's trustworthy love in your life?

5. Dr. Matheson highlights the fact that our brains are our constant companion (page 28). They provide us with our ability to connect with God and others. Our brains both protect us and get us into trouble. Our brains are where our emotions, thoughts, and behaviors begin and end. Most of us take our brains for granted. What do you learn about yourself as you compare how you care for and develop your brain compared with how Jesus cared for and developed His brain?

6. After reading about the emotional cycle on page 39, what are your thoughts regarding the differences between guilt and shame?

7. As you explore development of your brain, why do you think it is critical to focus on vertical integration first?

8. What is your biggest takeaway from Chapters 2 and 3 of *YFB*? How will you use it to impact your life today?

_____

_____

_____

✠ ACCEPT

I (Gina) must admit, there have been a few times in my life when I felt like Carol—confused, "disconnected" from myself. Although our stories are different, like Carol, I experience similar emotional reactions. The harassment and subsequent disintegration of her brain that Carol endured led her to experience regret, guilt, and embarrassment, ultimately leading to shame.

Such shame is corrosive to our story (page 40). Reintegration with God is the key. When Jesus says, "Love the Lord your God with all your heart and with all your soul and with your entire mind. This is the first and greatest commandment. And the second is like it: Love your neighbor as yourself" (Matt. 22:37–39, CSB), He gives us direction to the inseparable qualities of loving God, loving others, and loving ourselves. But it must start with vertical integration (remember, vertical integration starts with God and leads to the integration of our brain, heart, and nervous system).

In Chapter 3, we discussed the importance of integration and how sin in our lives creates dis-integration. As for our own sin, God has been gracious to give us signs within our own minds and bodies that we are out of step with His created reality. But we need to learn to pay attention to these. Remember, as Dr. Matheson said, "The sufficiency of our horizontal brain integration (the integration of the left and right hemispheres of the brain) depends on how well we develop our vertical integration" (page 36). The blessing is that because of God's grace, we have the opportunity to re-integrate with His created reality at any given moment.

Practically speaking, how do we learn to recognize when our vertical integration is off? Simply put, brain dis-integration is the underlying cause of most emotional troubles and interpersonal strife (page 37). If you are experiencing some sort of confusion pertaining to choices or relationships, there is a good chance you may be dealing with some vertical dis-integration.

This is not necessarily a willful decision we make; it could be something brought about by inadvertently leaving God out of the equation. In any case, re-integration will be key to helping you deal with those challenges. The place to begin is inviting God into your situation. Even if this starts with asking for His help in trusting Him more, that's okay! He's big enough to handle it and desires that sort of authenticity from us.

Take an inventory today. Are there areas or relationships in your life that are bringing about confusion for you? Invite God into those areas. Listen to what He has to say. This may seem awkward at first, and it may feel like you can't hear Him. But keep leaning in! Just like other relationships we have, it takes time to recognize someone's "voice" in a crowd. And if your world is anything like mine, there are a lot of "voices," making for a very loud and crowded space. Be particularly aware of when one (or more) of those voices is shame. It will drive you from the safety of connection, including connection with God. It may tell you that "you are beyond help or hope." But that's a lie meant to keep you from experiencing the healing and hope God has for you that will ultimately turn you into the powerhouse He's created you to be.

Scripture is a good way to discover what God's "voice" sounds like. We often suggest that people try a few different versions of the Bible in order to find a translation that speaks to them in the clearest way. Biblegateway.com is a great place to explore the same verse from a variety of translations. Try incorporating Psalm 139 (a great Psalm to promote vertical integration) as you take the time to pray and ponder God's great love for you. He will be faithful to meet you in the midst of it.

"If we do not fill minds with guilt and self-recriminations, we will recognize our incompleteness as a kind of spaciousness into which we can welcome the flow of grace."

—Gerald G. May

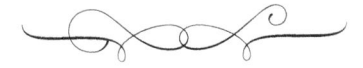

4

A faithful brain is
RELATIONAL

I GIVE THEM A LIFE THAT IS UNCEASING, AND DEATH WILL NOT HAVE THE LAST WORD. NOTHING OR NO ONE CAN STEAL THEM FROM MY HAND.
—John 10:28 (The Voice)

"WITH GOD IT'S NOT ABOUT BEHOLDING LIFE, BUT BEING HELD OURSELVES IN THE ACT OF BEHOLDING IT."
—Craig D. Lounsbrough

Our brains are designed to be relational. We function best when we are in healthy relationships, including our relationship with God. It is impossible to fully explore what it means to develop a faithful brain without discussing the importance of a relationship with God.

Our brains form deeper connections within itself as we relate with God through both our emotions and thoughts, using both our right and left hemispheres to engage spiritually. In Chapter 4 of *YFB*, we learn how God uses both thoughts and emotions to give us a fuller understanding of Scripture and to deepen our faith.

▶ **Read *A Faithful Brain is Relational*, Chapter 4 of *YFB*.**

ASSESS

Circle the number that best describes your thoughts, opinions, and feelings about each statement.

1 - - - - -2- - - - -3- - - - - 4- - - - -5- - - - - 6

| *Disagree* | *Disagree* | *Disagree* | *Agree* | *Agree* | *Agree* |
| *Completely* | *Somewhat* | *Slightly* | *Slightly* | *Somewhat* | *Completely* |

1. **Having faith in God means being confident in my relationship with Him.**

   1 - - - - -2- - - - -3- - - - - 4- - - - -5- - - - - 6

2. **Sometimes, language seems insufficient for me to communicate how I'm thinking and feeling.**

   1 - - - - -2- - - - -3- - - - - 4- - - - -5- - - - - 6

3. A relationship with Jesus is an opportunity to understand the Bible more personally and deeply.

1— — — — —2— — — — —3— — — — —4— — — — —5— — — — —6

4. I have experienced love as a transformative power that makes healing possible.

1— — — — —2— — — — —3— — — — —4— — — — —5— — — — —6

5. Most of my strongest memories have an emotional component to them.

1— — — — —2— — — — —3— — — — —4— — — — —5— — — — —6

6. My brain is designed for relationships.

1— — — — —2— — — — —3— — — — —4— — — — —5— — — — —6

Write out the statement you **agree** with most. _____

_____

_____

Why do you agree with this particular statement more than the others?

_____

_____

_____

Write out the statement you **disagree** with most. _____

_____

_____

Why do you disagree with that particular statement more than the others?

_____

_____

_____

_____

"Greater love has no one than this; to lay down one's life for his friends."

—John 15:13 (ESV)

= ALIGN

> "ANY MAN COULD, IF HE WERE SO INCLINED, BE THE SCULPTOR OF HIS OWN BRAIN."
>
> —Santiago Ramón y Cajal

Our brains work best when we integrate the various functions. For instance, when we utilize both hemispheres of our brains: the logic/language of the left brain with the emotion/experience of the right brain. When we bring this type of integration into our relationship with God, we are able to experience His presence in a deeper way. This short story from Rick Warren sketches out nicely the importance of brain integration in our relationship with God.

Rick tells a story of when he decided to pray and give his life to Christ. After studying the claims of Jesus and believing them, he prayed a prayer of salvation, a commitment to believing and following Him.

Rick described some of the details of his prayer; then, he asked a rather surprising question to those of us listening: "After I prayed that very sincere prayer, do you know what I felt?"

I was waiting for some incredible retelling of his experience. But instead, he answered his own question with this:

"I felt absolutely nothing."

Why? Why would he have no significant change in his feelings if his prayer was so sincere? First and foremost, it's true that a commitment to and relationship with Christ isn't all about feelings.

But we believe Rick's story is a great example of the importance of integrating both hemispheres of our brain. Rick had the left-brain experiences of logically deciding to accept the claims of Jesus and speaking his prayer of salvation, but he hadn't yet experienced the right-hemisphere engagements, which provide a deeper level of interaction with God's love, grace, and mercy. Rick's brain had to become integrated in how it interacted to fully experience God.

In this section, we have designed two activities (Part A and Part B) to facilitate brain integration in our relationship with God. Part A is engaging the left hemisphere of your brain. When thinking left brain, think: **logic, language, linear**. Part B is engaging the right hemisphere of your brain. When thinking right brain, think: **creativity, melody, gist, aesthetic**. The idea is to connect with God in a more integrated way, to experience Him more fully with our brains as He designed us to do. Experiencing God is done best as a "whole-brained" activity. Usually, we find that we are more dominant in one hemisphere. These exercises are designed to help you engage and develop both hemispheres so that integration becomes more natural.

PART A: ACTIVITY THAT DRIVES LEFT-BRAIN ENGAGEMENT

As we learned in this chapter, incorporating the whole brain in the study of Scripture enhances its meaning and impact on our lives. Dr. Matheson suggests reading the statement "God is Love" out loud, using a different vocal emphasis on each word (page 63). Now, let's take that exercise to Scripture. Select one of your favorite Bible verses (if you don't have any, you can use any found in this book or Google "favorite Bible passages" and pick one) and write it in the space provided below. Then read it aloud, selecting different words to place vocal emphasis on. Pay attention to how this impacts your understanding of God and His Word. The meaning will expand as your emphasis shifts on a word-by-word basis, working your way through each sentence.

_____

_____

_____

_____

_____

_____

> "Your brain was designed for relationships, beginning with a confident relationship with God, also known as faith."
>
> — Len Matheson

PART B: ACTIVITY THAT DRIVES RIGHT-BRAIN ENGAGEMENT

What are some of the ways in which you connect with God? For some, it is time spent in nature, others like to listen to music, and some find that exercising or creating is a sort of "spiritual language" for them.

I (Gina) have a hard time choosing. My most consistent ways of experiencing and connecting with God are often found in nature and music, although I'm often drawn to expressing my love and connection with God through writing, painting, and even in certain forms of exercise, like dance.

I (Dondra) find deep experiences with God in nature, time with loved ones, and in creating. Journaling and creating in the written word offer up opportunities to connect with God as well. Like Gina, the ways in which I connect with and experience God are not static. They are fluid and can change based on what God is revealing to me and in what particular season of life I find myself.

When our right brain is engaged, there will be a greater experience of awe, wonder, and emotional connection with the Lord—being overcome emotionally in a positive way. **Awe** is a deepening awareness of God's awe-someness as we sometimes experience it in nature, such as being at the ocean, standing by the Grand Canyon, seeing thousands of stars in the sky, etc. This awe engages our right brain by helping us to *feel,* rather than just to know intellectually, the magnitude (the "huge" reality) of who God is. What inspires this for each of us differs somewhat. As such, you will have your own ways to connect with God that may not be listed here. Take time to explore what helps create that sense of awe for you.

Spend some time practicing your "spiritual language," and when possible, combine this with reading or reciting your chosen Scripture. The goal here is to integrate the left and right brain to deepen your experience of God. Pay attention to how these activities further enhance your relationship with Him. Use the space below to record some of your experiences throughout this exercise.

_____

_____

_____

_____

_____

➡ ACCELERATE

1. "Your relationship with God is the template for your relationships with others" (page 51). How have you seen that in your own life? In what ways does this idea challenge you? In what ways does this idea provide guidance to you?

   _____
   _____
   _____

2. What stood out to you in Charlie's story (pages 52–56)? His pain, confusion, and inability to deal with his memories? Perhaps his reactions—his irritability, his withdrawal from his loved ones, his inability to relax and rest? How have you experienced some of these things in your own life?

   _____
   _____
   _____

3. "One of the most important characteristics of your brain is how it intertwines language, thoughts, and emotions" (page 57). This combination of language, thoughts, and emotions can be confusing at times, like it was for Charlie. What are some of your recent experiences that feel confusing, upsetting, or even painful for you?

   _____
   _____
   _____

4. We remember things that have emotional salience (thoughts attached to feelings). What are some ways you can engage Scripture so that it has more emotional salience for you?

_____

_____

_____

_____

5. "Our brains are designed to do best when we're in loving and trusting relationships with others" (page 71). Who in your life can you count on to be there for you? (Perhaps consider sharing something you are learning in this study to further enhance your relationship.)

_____

_____

_____

_____

6. In what ways are you experiencing God as a trusted friend, a safe and loving relationship for you? In what ways might this be difficult for you?

_____

_____

_____

_____

7. Being able to emotionally engage with the biblical narrative comes through your relationship with Jesus and your connections with others in your church community. Is there someone you feel God might desire for you to connect with more deeply? (This could be a loved one, a trusted friend, or someone you just met). What could you do to take a step in that direction today?

_____

_____

_____

8. What is your biggest takeaway from Chapter 4 of *YFB*? How will you use it to impact your life today?

_____

_____

_____

✝ ACCEPT

> "Taste and see that the Lord is good; blessed is the one who takes refuge in him."
>
> —Psalm 34:8 (NIV)

As we take a deeper look at the importance of recognizing how thoughts and feelings are intertwined, it is important to consider how this impacts us personally. In reading Charlie's story, it would be easy to become swept up in his circumstances. After all, it is a story straight from the headlines. We can easily think that because of the gravity of his situation, the impact on his brain was exceptional. But just like Charlie, our brains run the risk of, or perhaps have already experienced, the ordeal of being hijacked by trauma. Whether something along the lines of what Charlie went through, or what we would consider more common struggles like loss, divorce, or illness, the key to healing is integrating our faith through the engagement of our whole brain into the process of drawing closer to God.

On page 51, Dr. Matheson gives us another definition of faith to consider. He calls it "a confident relationship with God." This is a powerful thought. When we are unable to have confidence in others or in how something may turn out, having faith in God is critical. Without it, we cannot fully use our brains to interact with God. Words on a page become no more than ink and paper. The deeper meaning and, consequently, transformative potential for healing is lost if we do not allow it to penetrate our minds fully. This kind of faith is the building block of resilience, all done in the context of a relationship with Jesus. We need to pay attention to the "relational" emphasis here because our relational brain can help restore God's meaning to His written Word (page 63).

In John 1:1, we have the personal aspect of Jesus defined for us: "The Word was *with* God and the Word *was* God." The Word being capitalized here gives us a clue. It is more than spoken or written language here, the Word is a *person*: Christ Himself. Think of it another way. God knew we needed relationship for true and lasting change to occur in our lives. He designed us that way, and Jesus came to fulfill the ultimate form of relationship for us, knowing our brains would need this relationship to develop wholly.

The brain plays an important part in our resilience. This, in turn, impacts us on all other levels of our functionality. But the level of resilience we can experience is directly impacted by our ability to have trusting relationships with others. Ultimately, we want God to be at the forefront when it comes to trusting and loving relationships in our lives. But sometimes we've experienced great loss or trauma, and it can be difficult to trust God. We may wonder where He was in the midst of it all. Or, worse yet, we may have suffered something painful at the hands of someone who professed to be a lover of God. Regardless of how our relationship and ability to trust Him has been negatively impacted, it is important to work through this.

Get help from someone you *do* trust, someone who isn't looking to give you canned answers or make you feel worse about your fear in trusting God, but rather, someone who can help you work through those struggles, recognizing that sometimes in our finiteness, we won't be able to get all the answers we want. But we can still have a relationship with God and work out the rest of our struggles within the context of that relationship, recognizing that His heart grieves with and for us in the midst of our pain.

When we experience the kind of relationships that offer us a space of safety, free of shame and thick with connection, we handle stress better, we're less susceptible to infections and disease, and we can recover from trauma better. God can and desires to provide that kind of relationship with us.

The deeper we dive into the waters of developing a faithful brain, the more we will see the impact it has on us: body, mind, and soul. Today, ask God to help you lean into His trustworthiness and His love. Engage fully with Him and His Word so you can feel, hear, taste, smell, and see the benefits in all aspects of your life.

"I HAD STRUGGLED SO HARD AND SO LONG THAT I HAD SIMPLY EXHAUSTED MYSELF, ONLY TO FIND THAT GOD HAD ALL THE TIME IN THE WORLD TO WAIT FOR ME TO ALLOW HIM TO FREE ME."

—Michelle McKinney Hammond

5

A faithful brain is
REHABILITATIVE

"Grace isn't just forgiveness, it is forgiveness fueled by surrender."

—Amy E. Spiegel

So let us step boldly to the throne of grace, where we can find mercy and grace to help when we need it most.

—Hebrews 4:16 (The Voice)

How we make sense of our emotional reactions either leads to brain growth and rehabilitation or to disintegration and disconnection. God uses "corrective emotions" to help us recalibrate our lives, but these emotions can also lead us to shut down if we respond with self-judgment and condemnation rather than with grace and surrender.

Repeated throughout this chapter of this guidebook, you will find the message that grace and surrender are inseparable. As you read through Chapters 5 and 8 of *YFB*, you will see for yourself how grace and surrender work together through neuroplasticity to engender brain growth. Come see how this leads to growth in your character and quality of life.

▶ **Read *A Faithful Brain Is God-Rehabilitated* (Chapter 5) and *A Faithful Brain Is Grace-Blessed* (Chapter 8) of *YFB*.**

ASSESS

"In the beginning was the Word, and the Word was with God and the Word was God."

—John 1:1 (NIV)

Circle the number that best describes your thoughts, opinions, and feelings about each statement.

1– – – – –2– – – – –3– – – – –4– – – – –5– – – – – 6

Disagree   Disagree   Disagree   Agree   Agree   Agree
Completely   Somewhat   Slightly   Slightly   Somewhat   Completely

1. **Engaging in learning about science will grow my faith toward the unlimited nature of God.**

   1– – – – –2– – – – –3– – – – –4– – – – –5– – – – – 6

2. **Receiving God's grace is what makes surrender to Him possible.**

   1– – – – –2– – – – –3– – – – –4– – – – –5– – – – – 6

3. My brain has been designed for redemption and rehabilitation.

   1- - - - -2- - - - -3- - - - - 4- - - - -5- - - - - 6

4. I ask God for grace and forgiveness on a regular basis.

   1- - - - -2- - - - -3- - - - - 4- - - - -5- - - - - 6

5. The pain I have experienced in my life has brought me closer to God.

   1- - - - -2- - - - -3- - - - - 4- - - - -5- - - - - 6

6. Because I have accepted God's grace and forgiveness, I have been able to forgive myself.

   1- - - - -2- - - - -3- - - - - 4- - - - -5- - - - - 6

7. Because I have accepted God's grace and forgiveness, I have been able to forgive others.

   1- - - - -2- - - - -3- - - - - 4- - - - -5- - - - - 6

Write out the statement that you **agree** with most. _____

_____

_____

Why do you agree with this particular statement more than the others?

_____

_____

_____

_____

Write out the statement that you **disagree** with most. _____

_____

_____

Why do you disagree with that particular statement more than the others?

_____

_____

_____

_____

"Define yourself radically as one beloved by God. This is the true self. Every other identity is illusion."

—Brennan Manning

⊜ ALIGN

Reading through Chapters 5 and 8, we can see the bigger picture of how intricately surrender and grace are woven together. We also get a glimpse of how this impacts our brain development and our character development as we utilize Just-Right Challenges that help us develop our character and free us from the burden of shame.

In these exercises, our goal is to help you recognize the impact shame has had on your life and where it may have left you disconnected from others, God, and even from yourself.

PART A

Think about how shame has impacted your life. This can be difficult because shame is corrosive. It isn't an experience we want to intentionally conjure. It isn't something we "seek"—with good reason. Throughout the Bible, we see a message of Jesus taking away shame and exchanging it for His love and acceptance. Where shame told people like the tax collector, the woman at the well, and the woman caught in adultery that there was something wrong with *who* they were, Jesus recognized and, consequently, helped them to see that their problems were about *what* they had done. He saw *who* they were as valuable, lovable, and capable of making better choices that would help them find the full life that He offers.

What about you? Have you experienced a difference in how shame impacts your life since coming to know Christ's grace? If so, describe it here. If not, use this space to write a prayer asking God to help you experience His grace and forgiveness.

PART B

For some of us, the idea of certain emotions as "corrective emotions" may be new and even challenging. Remember, a "corrective emotion" is something we experience in light of our behaviors, thoughts, or responses being incongruent with what we say our values and beliefs are. When we are faced with values confusion (something we can't seem to fit within our constructs), it is very painful. As long as information is consistent with our values, it's easily organized and we experience understanding and a sense of congruency. But if the information (such as our own thoughts and behaviors) doesn't square with our values, it starts to create confusion.

We can experience a sort of dis-integration of our hearts and minds. When recognized swiftly, things like guilt or conviction can be beneficial to helping us realign our actions and values. When left unattended, this incongruence can result in intense feelings of destructive shame, depression, and anxiety and deepen the patterns of unhealthy choices.

Use this space to explore some areas in your life where God's grace has made it possible for you to learn and grow without debilitating shame. Perhaps you will want to reflect on a time when your behaviors were inconsistent with your values and God allowed you to experience a "corrective emotion" that helped you get back on track.

___

How have surrender and grace come into the picture for you as a result? How has this impacted the person you are in your daily life?

___

> "Jesus tapped me on the shoulder and said, 'Bob, why are you resisting me?' I said, 'I'm not resisting You!' He said, 'You gonna follow Me?' I said, 'I've never thought about that before!' He said, 'When you're not following Me, you're resisting Me."
>
> —Bob Dylan

➡ ACCELERATE

"Holding our story and loving ourselves through that process is the bravest thing that we will ever do."

—Brené Brown

1. What, if any, are the challenges you face with the idea of completely surrendering to God? What are some steps you can take to address those challenges?

   _____
   _____
   _____
   _____

2. One of my (Gina) favorite stories from *YFB* is the story of the Bach-y-Rita family (page 84). I see in this story there is a picture of both grace and surrender. Can you see it? What about this story is surprising to you? How does it lead you to think differently about your brain and how God created it?

   _____
   _____
   _____
   _____

3. What is your opinion of the statement, "The Bible should be part of medical scientists' undergraduate education" (page 86)? Expand on your opinion as much as possible. Cite some real-life examples if possible (i.e., what has informed your opinion?). If you are not doing this study in a group, find someone with whom you can discuss your opinion.

_____
_____
_____
_____

4. On page 81, we learn the importance of Just-Right Challenges for optimal brain development. What are some Just-Right Challenges you can set for yourself this week? Make a plan to do them and journal about your experience.

_____
_____
_____
_____

5. How have you experienced God's grace? Are there challenges you face with understanding or accepting His grace? Who can you process your answers with? Will you do that today?

_____
_____
_____
_____

6. Chapter 8 talks a great deal about "corrective emotions." After reading the information in the chapter, describe a time in your life when you experienced a corrective emotion. What were the results of that experience? How did your relationship with God come into play?

_____

_____

_____

_____

7. A portion of the lyrics to *Amazing Grace* are written out for us (page 147). Take a moment and read them. Really read them. Use your out loud voice. Sing them if you want (left-right brain integration). Then, either in the space below or on a separate sheet of paper, write how those lyrics apply to your own story. You can even write your own version of the song if you like. If you feel safe in doing so, find someone to share it. (You don't have to sing it if you don't want to, but it might be fun!)

_____

_____

_____

_____

8. What is your biggest takeaway from Chapters 5 and 8 of *YFB*? How will you use it to impact your life today?

_____

_____

_____

"You cannot fulfill God's purposes for your life while focusing on your own plans."

—Rick Warren

✞ ACCEPT

> "FOR BY GRACE YOU HAVE BEEN SAVED, THROUGH FAITH; AND THAT NOT OF YOURSELVES, IT IS THE GIFT OF GOD, NOT AS A RESULT OF WORKS, SO THAT NO MAN CAN BOAST."
> —Ephesians 2:8 (NIV)

Prayerful thought and selection go into creating a companion guidebook like this one. In addition to countless hours poring over the original material in *Your Faithful Brain*, we worked hard to seek out and develop additional information that would enhance your understanding of the original text as well as deepen the impact on the lives of those who interacted with it. When it came to examining the chapters of the book, deciding which should stand alone in the guidebook and which should be combined, one of the easiest decisions was combining Chapters 5 and 8. In both our professional and personal experiences, surrender is an insurmountable task unless done under the protection of God's grace. You might look at it this way: if surrender is the destination, then grace is the vehicle that gets us there.

So, why surrender? For what purpose? In Chapter 5, we are reminded that Paul teaches that surrender is necessary in order to be transformed by the renewing of our minds (Romans 12:2) through God's work in our lives. But we believe there's more. We believe an exceptionally important part of our transformation story occurs when we surrender to God the lies we believe about ourselves ("I'm too broken," "I don't deserve God," "I don't need God," etc.) and surrender to the truth of who we are created to be and who the living God is. This includes believing who He desires to be in our lives. Without grace, strong negative emotions cannot be corrective because we tend to protect ourselves when we feel attacked. What is intended to help us turns into emotions that shut us down and cause us to run farther from God rather than running into the safety and forgiving acceptance of His love. Without grace, they can only serve as a corrosive to our stories, trapping us in exaggerated lies about ourselves. With grace, we can grasp onto truths like, "There is no condemnation for those who are in Christ Jesus" (Romans 8:1, NIV). If we are rooted in such truths, the process of transformation becomes one less impeded by stress and fear. But, if we find ourselves stuck in patterns of shame and regret serving to defeat us rather than motivate us toward change and forgiveness, then we might need help in understanding what it looks like to experience God's grace and forgiveness.

For me (Gina), my history of abuse and trauma led me to make some incredibly self-destructive decisions in my life. For years, the shame of those decisions perpetuated a cycle of harm to myself and, at times, to others, which led to more shame, causing me to flee the safety of a relationship with God or anyone who reflected Him.

This makes me think of a quote from my friend and colleague, Polly Wright-Hamp. In her book, *Cherished: Shattered Innocence. Restored Hope*, she makes this profound observation: "The war against me and the war against you is about lies. The enemy knows that if he can get us to agree with those lies and believe that we are worthless or unlovable or damaged, we will make destructive choices."

I believed that I was too far gone and that anyone who *really* knew me knew what I had done or what had been done to me would deem me unworthy of love or acceptance. Ironically, that was the very thing that would heal me.

It wasn't until God placed some people in my life who wouldn't give up and who showed me Jesus that things began to change. With their help and the help of qualified Christian counseling, I began to discover who I truly am and that I am truly loved. Through this part of my journey, I found the courage to seek the help I needed to embrace the truth about myself and others.

Like so much of what God offers us, the benefits are more than spiritual and eternal. What He offers us is for the benefit of our entire being in this very moment and through into eternity. The key is trusting Him enough to believe He is for us and He will not abandon us. No. Matter. What!

If surrender has been a struggle for you, if shame has been corrosive in your life, and if God's grace seems like it is out of your reach, please consider praying for God's help today and seek the help of a clinically trained Christian counselor. Trust that God is patiently waiting for you and is willing to meet you where you are to help you become all you are created to be.

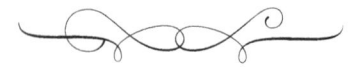

"So take seriously the story God has given you to live. It's time to read your own life, because your story is the one that could set us all ablaze."

—Dan Allender

6

A faithful brain is
TRUTH-GUIDED

From the beginning, creation in its magnificence enlightens us to His nature. Creation itself makes His undying power and divine identity clear, even though they are invisible; and it voids the excuses and ignorant claims of these people.
—Romans 1:20 (The Voice)

"We are either in the process of resisting God's truth or in the process of being shaped and molded by it."
—Charles Stanley

In order to pursue growth in the integration of our mind, heart, and spirit, an important area that needs our attention is our character. To do this well, it is essential that we recognize what truth we embrace and bring it under God's direction. This is the foundation upon which we build our values, which in turn leads to optimal brain functioning and organization. Investigate Chapters 9 and 10 to see how God's truth helps us avoid chaos and confusion.

▶ Read *A Faithful Brain Is Truth-guided* (Chapter 9) and *A Faithful Brain Is Organized by God* (Chapter 10) of *YFB*.

⧗ ASSESS

"The story we tell ourselves most often is the one that becomes most true."

—Gina Birkemeier

Circle the number that best describes your thoughts, opinions, and feelings about each statement.

1 – – – – –2– – – – –3– – – – – 4– – – – –5– – – – – 6

| Disagree | Disagree | Disagree | Agree | Agree | Agree |
| Completely | Somewhat | Slightly | Slightly | Somewhat | Completely |

1. **I am aligning my personal truth with God's truth.**

   1 – – – – –2– – – – –3– – – – – 4– – – – –5– – – – – 6

2. **I have noticed that when I choose my way over God's way, I often get bad results.**

   1 – – – – –2– – – – –3– – – – – 4– – – – –5– – – – – 6

3. There is a difference in believing in God versus allowing Him to guide our lives.

   1 - - - - -2- - - - -3- - - - - 4- - - - -5- - - - - 6

4. There is a difference in believing in God versus abiding in God.

   1 - - - - -2- - - - -3- - - - - 4- - - - -5- - - - - 6

5. The truth you embrace is the foundation of your values.

   1 - - - - -2- - - - -3- - - - - 4- - - - -5- - - - - 6

6. I have people in my life who consistently help me explore and live out my values.

   1 - - - - -2- - - - -3- - - - - 4- - - - -5- - - - - 6

7. My values are clear, strong, and, though a work in progress, seek to reveal Christ's character.

   1 - - - - -2- - - - -3- - - - - 4- - - - -5- - - - - 6

Write out the statement that you **agree** with most. _____

Why do you agree with this particular statement more than the others?

Write out the statement that you **disagree** with most. _____

Why do you disagree with that particular statement more than the others?

≡ ALIGN

Where we need to place our intentional focus of our character development can change based on the circumstances of our lives. We are often alerted to this need for character development when our behaviors misalign with what we say or think our values are. In the following exercise (and remainder of this chapter), we will emphasize the importance of building on a firm foundation of truth in order to work toward integration of mind and spirit.

PART A

You may remember this list from Chapter 3. In this chapter, we are going to use that same list for a different purpose. From the list of character traits below, choose one from each area of brain integration that you feel **a) is very important to you personally** and **b) is a strength you would like to strengthen in your life**. If you are struggling to choose, it may be helpful to think about what is most relevant to your circumstances at this point in life.

> "…your history of silence won't do you any good, did you think it would? Let your words be anything but empty. Why don't you tell them the truth?"
>
> —Sara Bareilles

Brain Integration	Character Strength
Vertical	Hope
Vertical	Appreciation
Vertical	Gratitude
Vertical	Humor
Vertical	Humility
Vertical	Mercy
Vertical	Self-Control
Vertical	Prudence
Vertical	Vitality
Vertical	Dependability
Vertical	Bravery
Vertical	Persistence
Horizontal	Curiosity
Horizontal	Open-mindedness
Horizontal	Love of Learning
Horizontal	Perspective
Horizontal	Creativity
Social	Love of Learning
Social	Kindness
Social	Social Intelligence
Social	Citizenship
Social	Fairness
Social	Leadership

EXAMPLE:

Vertical	*Self-Control*
Horizontal	*Love of Learning*
Social	*Kindness*

Vertical   _____

Horizontal _____

Social   _____

PART B

Now, write down the definition of the strength you chose.

Hint: Use whatever resources you have available (online dictionaries, websites, books, etc.) to help you find a definition for each word or phrase.

EXAMPLE:

Vertical	*Self-Control – the ability to control one's emotions and desires in difficult situations*
Horizontal	*Love of Learning – cultivating the passion and practice of continual learning*
Social	*Kindness – being friendly, generous, and considerate*

Vertical   _____

Horizontal _____

Social   _____

PART C

You may have already guessed what is next. For each of the strengths/virtues that you have chosen, what is one thing you could intentionally do this week to practice that strength? Write down your ideas below. Consider putting a reminder somewhere to help you remember your goals (on your bathroom mirror, in your calendar, in your phone—electronic reminders can be helpful).

EXAMPLE:

Vertical	*Self-Control – Learn a practice of deep breathing. Start the day by taking four deep breaths. I am committed to using this practice when I become stressed or anxious.*
Horizontal	*Love of Learning – Read from a source or about a topic I do not typically read, I find challenging, or I want to learn more about. I am committed to reading daily.*
Social	*Kindness – Hold the door for others and greet others throughout the day. I am committed to doing this daily.*

Vertical _____

_____

_____

Horizontal _____

_____

_____

Social _____

_____

_____

➡ ACCELERATE

> "Vulnerability sounds like truth and feels like courage. Truth and courage aren't always comfortable, but they're never weakness."
>
> —Brené Brown

1. "Character is revealed in the patterns of our behaviors. But the relationship between character and behavior is not simply circular; it's a spiral over time" (page 156). What do you think this statement means?

   _____

   _____

   _____

   _____

2. "Without values, we're left with only desires to guide us" (page 157). Describe a time in your life when your desires were driving you. How did it work out for you?

   _____

   _____

   _____

   _____

3. "Quality of life develops over time as we make the person and teachings of Jesus central to our lives." Has this been true for you? If so, how? If not, name a way that you would be willing to explore the teachings of Jesus and apply them to your life.

   _____
   _____
   _____
   _____

4. "Every good relationship is challenging and requires commitment and work because we're all broken in unique ways" (page 152). What does this statement mean to you?

   _____
   _____
   _____
   _____

5. What relationship in your life might benefit from a deeper level of commitment and work? Since you can't control the other person, what do you think God is asking of you in this relationship? As you consider this, try not to use the grid of "If I do this, then the other person will do . . ." Simply ask God to reveal to you what it is He's asking of you.

   _____
   _____
   _____
   _____

6. "When a person comes into my office in deep emotional pain, the most common cause is values confusion" (page 167). Values confusion means that something is misaligned in our emotional reactions, behaviors, and thoughts in relation to what we say our values are. Quickly assess your alignment: Are there areas that might be out of alignment? Can you name them?

_____
_____
_____
_____

7. "Prayers of surrender engage my entire being to such an extent that my intertwined thoughts and feelings are clarified by values not yet wholly my own" (page 172). Take a moment to write down a prayer of surrender here or on another piece of paper or in your journal. Start with, "Lord, I am trying to trust you more with my whole self. I surrender . . ." If you're having trouble with this, be honest about what is getting in the way and use that as part of your prayer.

_____
_____
_____
_____

8. What is your biggest takeaway from Chapters 9 and 10 of *YFB*? How will you use it to impact your life today?

_____

_____

_____

_____

ACCEPT

In our world today, truth can be a challenging subject to discuss. We find ourselves bombarded with a variety of truths. "Your truth is right for you, and mine is right for me" seems to be the guiding rule. But if truth is the foundation of our values and beliefs, and our values and beliefs help to form the organization of our brains, how sturdy of a foundation can be built on an ever-shifting perception of truth? And how firmly can we stand upon this foundation if it must constantly conform to fit the whims of relationships, the latest trends, or even our own fickleness? And if our values influence our thoughts and emotions and play out in our behavior, where can we go to find the stability and consistency that is necessary for optimal brain and character development?

It's important that we find an answer to this question. Without a stable foundation of truth, we will continue to be tossed about by shifting opinion and perspective. A reliable source of ultimate truth is required in order to repair the divide within ourselves. Much like we cannot build a house on an ever-shifting foundation, we cannot repair and build an integrated self, optimal for life to the full in line with God's created reality without beginning on solid ground.

For those of us no longer content with an ever-shifting, ambiguous form of truth, God offers an unchanging, dependable truth. In Jesus this truth is personified. In John 14:6 (NIV), He tells us, "I am the way, the *truth*, and the life. No one comes to the Father except through me." Each of us must answer for ourselves the question that Pastor Rick Warren presents regarding this verse: "Is Jesus making a threat or offering a promise?" When we are ready to embrace His truth as a promise, the foundation for healthy brains and lives are being set.

In Chapter 9, Dr. Matheson tells us that "character is the consistent behavioral presentation of our underlying values. It is how we are known." When our values and character are displayed through our behaviors, established and organized on the foundation of God's truth, our brains are less likely to be dis-integrated by chaos and confusion.

Because the foundation of God's truth is so unshakable, we are safe to grow from any corrective emotions that God may allow to enter into our circumstances. When we are firmly in His grasp, we can be certain that "neither death nor life, neither angels nor demons, neither our fears for today nor our worries about tomorrow—not even the powers of hell can separate us from God's love" (Romans 8:38, NLT). Living confidently in this truth will change the way we live and love God, others, and, ultimately, ourselves.

"The way I see it, putting your faith in God is something that each person has gotta come to on his or her own. It's your own personal relationship with Him; a bond that is as unique as a fingerprint."

—Bethany Hamilton

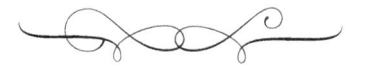

7

A faithful brain is
BALANCED

This is what the lord says: "Stand at the crossroads and look; ask for the ancient paths, ask where the good way is, and walk in it, and you will find rest for your souls . . ."
—Jeremiah 6:16 (NIV)

"I will call upon Your name and keep my eyes above the waves. When oceans rise, my soul will rest in your embrace, for I am Yours and You are mine."
—Hillsong

We all experience uncertainty at times. Fear grips us; we waver in our faith. This chapter helps us grapple with these fears, teaching us that coming to rest in God's safe love provides us not only temporary emotional relief, but also long-lasting effects on how our hearts and brains connect and communicate. By inviting God into the process, we maximize the connection between our hearts and brains.

▶ **Read *A Faithful Brain Is Heart-Balanced* (Chapter 6) of *YFB*.**

ASSESS

"Go where your best prayers take you."
—Frederick Buechner

Circle the number that best describes your thoughts, opinions, and feelings about each statement.

1 – – – – –2– – – – –3– – – – – 4– – – – –5– – – – – 6

Disagree Completely   *Disagree Somewhat*   *Disagree Slightly*   *Agree Slightly*   *Agree Somewhat*   *Agree Completely*

1. **Caring for my body is a spiritual responsibility as well as a physical one.**

    1– – – – –2– – – – –3– – – – –4– – – – –5– – – – – 6

2. **I have been designed to be a fully integrated being.**

    1– – – – –2– – – – –3– – – – –4– – – – –5– – – – – 6

3. I have experienced less anxiety in my life by resting in the *safe* love of God.

   1– – – – –2– – – – –3– – – – – 4– – – – –5– – – – – 6

4. Prayer may not always change my circumstances, but prayer does change me.

   1– – – – –2– – – – –3– – – – – 4– – – – –5– – – – – 6

5. Human beings are *designed* for relationships.

   1– – – – –2– – – – –3– – – – – 4– – – – –5– – – – – 6

6. When my morality is uncertain, my ability to love is limited.

   1– – – – –2– – – – –3– – – – – 4– – – – –5– – – – – 6

Write out the statement you **agree** with most. _____

_____

_____

Why do you agree with this particular statement more than the others?

_____

_____

_____

_____

Write out the statement you **disagree** with most. _____

_____

_____

Why do you disagree with that particular statement more than the others?

_____

_____

_____

_____

⊜ ALIGN

> "PEACE I LEAVE WITH YOU; MY PEACE I GIVE YOU. I DO NOT GIVE TO YOU AS THE WORLD GIVES. DO NOT LET YOUR HEARTS BE TROUBLED AND DO NOT LET THEM BE AFRAID."
>
> —John 14:27 (ESV)

Chapter 6 of *YFB* discusses the links between our hearts and brains. We learn that damage can be done to these links through a variety of sources. On page 105, Dr. Matheson shares with us the beginnings of his journey to healing those damaged heart-brain links. His vagal nervous system needed to be returned to a healthy tone so the heart-brain connection could help put him back into emotional balance.

For Dr. Matheson, the Third-Step Prayer of Dr. Bob, a founder of Alcoholics Anonymous, helped him get started (see pages 105–106). The Third Step of AA says they *"made a decision to turn our will and our lives over to the care of God, as we understood Him."*

In light of the Third Step and Dr. Bob's prayer, write your own prayer of actively turning your will and life over to God. Think in terms of what is impacting your heart-brain connection and how you want God to intervene in the process.

_____

_____

_____

_____

➡ ACCELERATE

1. Think of a time when you clearly felt your emotions physically in your body. In that situation, what was the emotion? Where did you feel it? Were you able to recognize the physical symptoms you were experiencing as coming from your emotions? If you shared your experience at the time, what was the outcome of sharing (e.g., feeling better, feeling worse, finding more clarity, etc.)?

   _____

   _____

   _____

   _____

2. On pages 96 and 97 of *YFB*, we are introduced to the idea of our brains having what is known as "negative response bias." List something that you had to "train your brain" not to fear. (Example: as a child, I feared dogs; now I no longer fear them.) Discuss the process.

   _____

   _____

   _____

   _____

3. What "automatic thoughts" (Beck, 1967) in your life create difficulties in relationships (e.g., "People can't be trusted," "I'm not worthy of love," "I'm a failure")? What are some truths you can list to help combat those "automatic thoughts"? Make reciting these statements often a part of your "brain-training" exercise (e.g., "I have friends

who care about me," "Jesus died for me," "I may have failed, but I am not a failure").

_____

_____

_____

_____

4. In this *YFB* chapter, we explored the vagus nerve tone, which "improves when you experience loving and trusting relationships" (page 102). Reflecting on relationships in your own life, share an experience when you felt the impact of a loving relationship on your mood or state of mind.

_____

_____

_____

_____

5. When morality and ethics lack a strong and healthy foundation, uncertainties can develop that have the potential to be dangerous to ourselves and our world. List some ways in which you see this being played out in our world today. How does this connect to us being created for loving relationships with one another?

_____

_____

_____

_____

6. In light of your answers to the previous question, name one way you can get involved to promote positive change. How will this be a relational endeavor?

   _____
   _____
   _____
   _____

7. In what ways would you like to improve your heart-brain connection? How do you think this would impact your relationships?

   _____
   _____
   _____
   _____

8. What is your biggest takeaway from Chapter 6 of *YFB*? How will it impact your life moving forward?

   _____
   _____
   _____
   _____

✟ ACCEPT

> "It is not good for the man to be alone."
> —Genesis 2:18 (NIV)

I (Gina) didn't understand the full scope of this Scripture until I went to seminary. Not that it wasn't important to me or that I didn't see the beauty in God providing for Adam. I was just unaware of the weight of this Scripture in light of how we've been created.

I don't mean the "how" as in the physical, biological mechanisms that are a part of us. Rather, how this Scripture points us to the idea that we've been created *for* relationship. Scripture tells us that God said, "Let us make mankind in *our* image, in *our* likeness" and "God created mankind in His own image, in the image of God He created them; male and female He created them" (Gen. 1:26a and 28, NIV). We are created in the image of ultimate relational perfection, the image of the Triune God. His image demonstrates for us the principles mentioned in Chapter 6. Complete trust and security, along with moral and ethical certainty, create a relationship in which each (Father, Spirit, Son) is able to fully experience and achieve what each desires.

While this is a picture of an all-encompassing perfection that we cannot achieve, it is, nonetheless, the image we've been created in. It also points us to what we've been created for. We even find clues and encouragement for this in Scripture. First Corinthians 11:1 encourages us to "be imitators of Christ." Ephesians 5:1 reminds us to "be imitators of God, as beloved children." And finally, in Galatians 5:25, we read, "If we live by the Spirit, let us also walk by the Spirit." These verses give us guidance. If we read each of the passages more fully, we find that each speaks to relationship with God, with others, and with ourselves.

The idea that we are created in the image of a relational God explains why we are hardwired for relationship. When God stated that "it is not good for man to be alone," He knew what Science would discover much later. Countless studies have been done over the years confirming what God knew from the beginning. We heal and grow and learn best in the context of relationship. This doesn't mean merely in romantic relationships, but in a context of all healthy relationships.

Unfortunately, relationship was tainted in the Fall (this is what we refer to when speaking of the story of Adam and Eve in the garden), and as a consequence, our overall well-being was impacted. We see it in the story of the garden. Once uncertainty and distrust entered the story, it paved the way for pain, betrayal, brokenness, and a whole host of destructive emotions and behaviors. The impact was beyond spiritual. The entire makeup of man was impacted. We call this the Science of the Fall.

What do we mean by the Science of the Fall? We tend to look at the Fall as a spiritual occurrence, but often we leave it at that. We think there is more to it. In Chapter 6, Dr. Matheson writes about our dis-integration from God, others, and, consequently, ourselves when we are in a place of uncertainty and insecurity. The Fall opened the door for us to be broken and harmed in the context of relationship. Sadly, it left the door open for us to hurt others too.

The dis-integration of key relationships (where uncertainty and distrust enter in) feeds negative pathways in our brain. This occurs in the brain and is played out in the body. When we "rehearse" these thoughts, they become the reality we operate from, impacting our overall well-being. This is what we believe is the Science of the Fall.

However, the good news is that while we are broken in the context of relationship, we are also healed in the context of relationship. God, in His infinite mercy, allowed the positive impact of relationship to remain post-Fall. As we learned in Chapter 6, calming our hearts and minds can be experienced in loving relationships. These positive relational experiences give us an opportunity to "change our narrative," replacing negative thoughts with positive ones. Those thoughts become behaviors and produce a new reality from which we interact with the world. And just as the negative thoughts impact our overall wellness, so do the positive ones. Particularly, as we model our character after that of Christ. This requires a balance of heart and mind. A cooperation between the two that moves us further into the process of being integrated rather than living in a divided chaotic state.

This is more than a take on positive psychology. This is a picture of redemption!

8

A faithful brain is
LOVING

"All you need is love."
—The Beatles

But the greatest of these is love.
—I Corinthians 13:13 (NIV)

In this final chapter of our guidebook, the emphasis is on how God has designed our brains to fit perfectly with the ultimate command He has given us to love Him and others as ourselves. We are created for the purpose of giving and receiving love. We are designed for relationship. When we are at our best, our brains are involved in loving God, ourselves, and others. It becomes about more than an emotional happenstance. It is an intentional, guided decision carried out in our actions and responses to the world around us.

Our brains respond to the giving and receiving of love by releasing neurochemicals like oxytocin, which decrease our stress responses and encourage us to deepen our trust and transparency with others. God has built within our brains a positive feedback loop, leading us to experience a more optimal life, the life He Himself designed for us to live.

▶ **Read *A Faithful Brain Is Loving* (Chapter 7) of *YFB*.**

ASSESS

Circle the number that best describes your thoughts, opinions, and feelings about each statement.

1- - - - -2- - - - -3- - - - - 4- - - - -5- - - - - 6

| Disagree | Disagree | Disagree | Agree | Agree | Agree |
| Completely | Somewhat | Slightly | Slightly | Somewhat | Completely |

1. **Loving God and loving others promotes brain growth and protection.**

    1- - - - -2- - - - -3- - - - - 4- - - - -5- - - - - 6

2. **Love must be secure and committed to offer its full benefits.**

    1- - - - -2- - - - -3- - - - - 4- - - - -5- - - - - 6

3. **I am committed to being in new covenant love relationships.**

    1- - - - -2- - - - -3- - - - - 4- - - - -5- - - - - 6

4. There is, at least, one person with whom I am completely transparent.

$$1-----2-----3-----4-----5-----6$$

5. Sharing my cares and concerns with others is something I do intentionally.

$$1-----2-----3-----4-----5-----6$$

6. I take the time to supportively listen to others' cares and concerns.

$$1-----2-----3-----4-----5-----6$$

Write out the statement that you **agree** with most. _____

_____

_____

Why do you agree with this particular statement more than the others?

_____

_____

_____

_____

Write out the statement that you **disagree** with most. _____

_____

_____

Why do you disagree with that particular statement more than the others?

_____

_____

> "The beauty of the covenant-keeping love between Christ and His church shines brightest when nothing but Christ can sustain it."
>
> —John Piper

ALIGN I

Next to our relationship with Christ, a loving marriage is the best way to experience new covenant love (page 115). New covenant love relationships give us a safe place to practice emotional risks. We can begin to experience relationship in a way that leaves us feeling secure and loved, even if we don't get our way. In essence, it is the experience of feeling unconditionally loved and accepted. These new covenant love relationships do not have to be just between spouses, although spouses should aspire to that kind of relationship.

PART A

List your closest relationships. Write something honest and transparent that you have told each person in the last few weeks.

_____

_____

_____

_____

_____

PART B

What was it like creating that list? For most of us, the risk of being open and transparent is challenging, maybe even shame-inducing ("What will people think if they know the truth about me?"). However, when we free ourselves through God's perfect love and acceptance, we can share more openly with others our fears, joys, failures, triumphs, and concerns.

What is something you haven't shared with anyone else that may be weighing you down right now?

_____

_____

_____

_____

_____

Make it a goal to share this with someone this week. If you can't think of anyone, tell Jesus and share with Him. Then, ask Him to bring someone into your life with whom you can be transparent.

= ALIGN II

Let's spend a little more time looking at the importance of loving, healthy relationships in our lives. Not only does Scripture indicate our "hardwiring" for these relationships, but Science does as well. It would seem that these relationships impact us physically, emotionally, mentally, *and* spiritually.

In her book, *Hold Me Tight,* Dr. Sue Johnson talks about the physical importance of loving relationships and the importance of oxytocin. She states that "oxytocin turns off our threat detector, the amygdala, as well as the hypothalamic-pituitary-adrenal (HPA) axis—the 'get up for challenge' part of our nervous system. It turns on the calming 'relax—all is fine' parasympathetic nervous system. The effect is reduced fear and anxiety and lower production of stress hormones."

She goes on to say that "researchers believe that oxytocin increases the release of dopamine (the neurotransmitter that makes us feel elated and euphoric) further supporting attachment between partners."

And in the event you would like a simpler, more straightforward message on the Science of loving relationships, Susan Pinker, in her book *The Village Effect: How Face-to-Face Contact Can Make Us Happier and Healthier,* says her research shows that "neglecting to keep in close contact with people who are important to you is at least as dangerous to your health as a pack-a-day cigarette habit, hypertension, or obesity."

There are a variety of studies and articles out there that outline the benefits of healthy, loving relationships, and we encourage you to do some exploration on this topic for yourself. Consider sharing your findings with those *you* love.

Find some scriptures that reflect the importance of and the ways in which we are created for loving relationships, including with God Himself. List two or three verses here.

_____

_____

_____

_____

_____

_____

_____

> "Love is not the opposite of power. Love IS power. Love is the strongest power there is."
>
> —Vironika Tugaleva

➡ ACCELERATE

> "Brain-renewal processes are promoted and protected by love."
> —Len Matheson

1. In light of what you read in Chapter 7 of *YFB*, how would you explain or describe the relationship between grace and risk?

   _____
   _____
   _____
   _____

2. Think of a time in your own life when you experienced firsthand the relationship between grace and risk. Now, at this point in your life, to whom do you need to extend grace so they can take risks in your relationship with them?

   _____

3. What are your thoughts regarding the difference between a contract marriage and a covenant marriage?

   _____
   _____
   _____
   _____

4. Think of a close relationship (if you are married, think about your spouse). Use the continuum below by placing an X on the line to indicate where you think the relationship is today. Using the same continuum, place an O where you want that same relationship to be.

Contract   **Covenant**
Relationship   **Relationship**

5. What are your reasons for placing each mark where you did?

_____

_____

_____

_____

6. Make a list here of something you can do today to begin moving your relationship toward a covenant relationship. (If your relationship is in distress, please consider getting help from a clinically trained Christian counselor who understands the concept of covenant relationships.)

_____

_____

_____

_____

_____

7. If you are able, initiate a conversation with your spouse/friend/family member about what you are learning. Be curious about their thoughts and desires for the relationship. Use this space to write some prompting questions, thoughts, ideas. (Perhaps plan a date night to set the stage for the conversation. Use this space to plan it out.)

_____

_____

_____

_____

8. What is your biggest takeaway from Chapter 7 of *YFB*? How will you use it to impact your life today?

_____

_____

_____

_____

✠ ACCEPT

"Love is patient, love is kind. Love does not envy, it does not boast, it is not proud. Love does not dishonor others, it is not self-seeking, it is not easily angered; it keeps no record of wrongs. Love does not delight in evil but rejoices with the truth. Love always protects, always trusts, always hopes, always perseveres. Love never fails."

— I Corinthians 13:4–8 (NIV)

To many of us, this is one of the best-known passages of Scripture. We hear it at weddings, renewing of vows, and sermons focused on the qualities of love. Yet, if we're honest, most of us pass over it as a noble ideal that can't wholly be attained, so we quickly dismiss it.

Or is it just me (Dondra)?

If I am the only one, you can skip down to the next paragraph. If you are still reading, I assume you have some similar struggles with this passage. Who can possibly "*always*" anything, much less *always* protect, *always* trust, *always* hope? And what about the patient part? I am pretty much out after this first descriptor as fast as I can read it.

For a long time, I thought of love as simply an emotion; if I love someone, I show them or tell them. But over the last several years, I have adapted my opinions about love. I still believe emotion is an important aspect of love, but I have learned that it is not always the emotion that leads to action but the other way around. This first lesson taught me that many times how I choose to treat someone, whether it be my spouse, my kids, my friends, or my dog, can affect how I feel about them. When I choose to appreciate the person's full value as established by God, not by my conditional assessment of them in the moment, I find I am better at showing them love as God designed. In other words, *I can act in love before I feel it.*

When my husband and I first got married, I thought if he loved me, he would show it by knowing what I needed and when. Surely, he would, at least, know when to say "I love you." But, apparently, love does not make you omniscient.

In order to experience more of the new covenant love that Len describes in Chapter 7, I have to take the risk to share with my husband what exactly it is that I am needing. This sounds not only obvious but also fairly straightforward. However, in my twenty-one years of marriage, I have not found it to be either.

First, it takes some work to figure out what it is that I am *really* needing. I also have to get real about his ability to give it to me (not all needs are meant to be fulfilled by a spouse. Or by another human for that matter). On the list of those things that qualify as realistic to seek from my husband, what I have found is that it often comes down to reassurance, support, validation—and occasionally, getting something off the top shelf.

Second, it takes courage (where practicing risk comes in) to ask for what I need. What if I ask, and he blows me off or doesn't respond or worse, criticizes me for it? These are serious and real fears for me. I have not had complete success overcoming these fears; however, I have noticed that at the times I am successful, I am experiencing God's love, reassurance, and support, which gives me the courage to reach out and risk potential rejection.

Now, we are going to ask you to be willing to risk. We are offering you two ways to respond.

If you need to take the first step of receiving reassurance of God's love: On an index card, write out I Corinthians 13:4–8 replacing the word "love" with "God" each time it appears and writing "with me, to me" or "for me" after each phrase. (Example: "*God* is patient *with me*, *God* is kind *to me*, etc.").

If you are ready to work on showing God's love more practically to others: On an index card, write out I Corinthians 13:4–8, replacing the word "love" with your own name each time it appears. (Example: "*Tom* is patient, *Tom* is kind.")

Now, place your card somewhere you will see it each day—on your bathroom mirror, the visor in your car, or your desk. Each day for thirty days, take the card out at least one time a day and read it aloud to yourself.

Make mental notes for when you are experiencing love from God or your spouse. Paying attention to positive evidences of love deepens those neural connections in our brains, creating a more robust overall experience of love in our lives. The idea here is that when we pay attention with our minds to what is happening in our spirits and hearts, we become more deeply integrated, not just as individuals but relationally as well.

Don't just take my word for it. Try it yourself!

> "To be loved but not known is comforting but superficial. To be known and not loved is our greatest fear. But to be fully known and truly loved is, well, a lot like being loved by God. It is what we need more than anything. It liberates us from pretense, humbles us out of our self-righteousness, and fortifies us for any difficulty life can throw at us."
>
> —Tim Keller

And just like that, we've reached the end of this particular journey together.

Congratulations! You made it!

We hope this has been an exciting and challenging journey into discovering what it means to have life to the full with God in the lead. As the result of the exercises and information in this guidebook and *YFB*, you've created new, healthy networks in your brain, improved your overall brain health, and, hopefully, deepened connections with God, others, and yourself.

Ultimately, you have improved your brain's integration! If you are open to sharing, we would love to hear about your experience. Please contact us at http://faithfulbrain.com/guidebook.

Still want more for your journey into optimal brain and character development? Check out the articles, blogs, and resources at http://faithfulbrain.com.

We hope that through the exercises and experiences provided in this guidebook, you've ignited your heart-brain connection at the intersection of Faith and Science. Perhaps along this journey, you've also found that joy isn't merely a state of emotion, rather, it can be and is best experienced as a state of our soul.

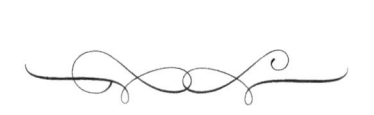

"Get on the road that's going to take you to the life you'll want to say you lived when you come to the end of it all."

—Beth Moore

APPENDIX A

Tips for Groups, Leaders & Facilitators

In this Appendix, you will find helpful ideas for exploring *Your Faithful Brain . . . Ignited!* in a group setting. We have included tips and hints for leaders/facilitators as well as other thoughts to help enrich your group experience.

Groups

Considering the personal and in-depth nature of the content and questions of this study, it is recommended that group size not exceed eight individuals (including the leader/facilitator) to allow for depth of processing.

While your attendance and participation is your most important contribution to the group, you will find a richer experience if you are able to complete the study prior to meeting. Whether you are the least or most likely to speak up during a group, everyone can tell their story and longs to tell it in a safe environment. We encourage you to take the risk. Share, and allow a safe place for those around you who are taking the same risk by holding their stories in confidence.

When beginning your group:

- Consider the role you want prayer to play in your group each time you meet.

- Discuss what feels safe for each person and how they would like others to respond to them when they share their stories.

- Talk about what each person is hoping to get from the study.

- Explore good experiences people have had in past groups that you could incorporate.

- Discuss start and stop times, length of group, being there on time, and other elements of the framework of the group.

Facilitator/Leader Guide

Thank you for your willingness to lead a study group! Don't worry, it isn't as scary as it sounds. For this study, you don't need to be a scientist or a pastor. A willing heart and mind will do just fine. Some general tips that might help you facilitate a healthy group are:

- Review chapter to highlight the activities and questions you would like the group to discuss before it meets.

- Select what you feel are key questions to encourage discussion (you will find additional help for this below).

- Remind the group that what is discussed stays within the confines of the group.

- Ask people to share how the chapter impacted them overall.

- Give everyone equal time to speak (you may need to call on people, but do so gently).

- Always give everyone a chance to share the takeaway question at the end of the Accelerate sections of each chapter.

- If someone seems to need an additional conversation, offer to speak with them outside of the group. You may need to consider having a resource list available of clinically trained Christian counselors or pastors in your area.

First Meeting/Kickoff

In our test group for this study, we found it helpful to have a kickoff meeting. You may want to do this for your group. We recommend you do this within a maximum of two weeks prior to your first group discussion. In your kickoff meeting, consider safe ways that group members can engage and begin to find a level of comfort with one another.

- Start with simple introductions, allowing each member to say as much or little about themselves as they would like. You can ask people to share what brought them to the group or what their interest is in this study.

- Play a fun icebreaker game:
  - One thing most people don't know about me is . . .
  - Fact or fiction: Each person writes two true things and one fiction about themselves. Read to group and ask members to decide which is which.
  - Build a story together: Have a person start with one sentence and each person adds a sentence from there to create a story. Predetermine the number of times you will go around the group.
  - Fill bowl with numbered pieces of paper (#2–4). Passing bowl, each person draws out a number and has to say that many things about themselves.
  - Speed dating: Each member has one minute each to talk with each other to get information. Continue until everyone has talked with each group member. Then, each person shares what they remember about the people in the group.

- Any other icebreakers you have used in previous groups.

- Get permission from group members to use their email for group communications. Gather email and any other needed contact info.

- Clearly communicate start and stop times and any additional logistical information that your group may need.

- Make sure everyone in the group has your contact information.

Leader Health

- Remember to give yourself time before and after group to pray and process your own thoughts and challenges from the group or study. Don't go it alone! This is a journey meant to be supported by those you love and trust.

- Take time to pray before group sessions for the Holy Spirit to bring out what He desires and to reduce the performance pressure you may be feeling.

- Work through the chapter/sections sufficiently ahead of time so you don't feel rushed or have to cram it all in right before group time.

- Give yourself time to rest after sessions and to reflect on how sessions went.

APPENDIX B

Definitions and Key Terms

Throughout this guidebook, you and your group will see unique terminology repeated. To give you a deeper understanding of what is being explored in the Accelerate sections, you may want to familiarize yourself with the following **key terms** and the intention behind the use of each. Refer back to this section to help yourself and others gain a clearer understanding of these concepts.

Science: When we say "Science," we're not talking about a disconnected, left-brained endeavor. Our hope is that through this book, you're able to see that Science isn't something that happens only in a lab, but rather is happening all around us, reflected in the grand design of a Creator who understands how all things are connected.

In this book, we're speaking of all the sciences that are integrated and apply to our discussion here. "Life to the full" requires intentionality and a holistic approach. So, when you hear "Science" within these pages, consider the following:

- **Interpersonal neurobiology:** How the brain and mind are shaped or developed and how they function based on the interplay of genes in the context of relationships.

- **Neuroscience:** Dealing with the structure or function of the nervous system and brain.

- **Psychology:** The study of the human mind, emotions, and their functions. Particularly how they affect behavior, choices, etc.

- **Physical science:** How the body functions, is structured, and also impacted by things outside of the physical world (spiritual, emotional, mental).

- **Faith:** For our purposes, faith is not from a specific religious tradition but the personal integration of biblical understanding with a relationship with God. It is at its most essential core the relationship one has with Jesus Christ based on the gift of salvation provided by Him on the cross.

- **Biblical understanding:** We are emphasizing a Reformed view, highlighting the broad themes of Creation, Fall, Redemption, and Restoration throughout Scripture as well as in the big picture of how God is working now in our lives.

- **Creation:** The way God originally designed our world, our work, our relationships, our bodies and minds, which was the perfect design.

- **Fall:** The great interruption of God's perfect design brought about by sin and rebellion, which threw into chaos His perfect order. The story can be found in Genesis, with its aftershocks portrayed throughout the remaining pages of Scripture and into our world today.

- **Redemption:** The recovery and rescue of God's people from their personal sins based on Jesus's perfect life, atoning sacrifice of death on the cross, resurrection from the dead, and ascension, offering his continual presence to His redeemed people through the Holy Spirit.

- **Restoration:** The return of God's perfect order and design, which is underway but will not be fully realized until Christ's return, ushering us into eternity. This restoration applies to *all* of creation.

- **Relationship with God:** Based on biblical understanding of our brokenness and personal acceptance of Jesus's atoning sacrifice, our restored relationship with the Father, Son, and Holy Spirit who relate to us as Three in One. This relationship is personal in that the Triune God relates to us as

Definitions and Key Terms

individuals in ways that connect with His design of us. We in turn relate to God through the ways in which we have been created.

- **Negativity Bias:** This is the tendency that the brain has toward self-protection. This automatic protection comes from the amygdala, the seat of our "fight or flight or freeze" response. Because this area of the brain registers warnings before we have a chance to think (cerebral cortex), it tends to be negative so that it can protect us. When we are faced with a challenge (new, different, anything that may be a threat), it sets off a protective reaction. This tendency does not discriminate among physical, relational, or emotional threats. It responds equally to any perceived threat. This negativity bias becomes problematic when our brains consistently register threats that aren't really there. This can happen for many reasons, often due to bad or traumatic experiences that cause us to become overly cautious with others or in certain situations.

- **Brain Redemption:** This begins when each of us surrenders to God, immediately optimizing the mechanisms that God designed in our brains throughout our development. Before Brain Redemption can occur, these mechanisms are in effect but not optimized because the "peace that passes all understanding" has not yet descended on the person, allowing for optimal Brain Redemption to unfold. "Peace that passes all understanding" isn't merely "happiness" as we may think of it in the everyday world, but rather an "it is well with my soul" kind of peace, even in the midst of circumstantial unrest. The brain is subjected to a variety of challenges and as a result, some neurons do not mature optimally, and some may even die, before taking their place to fully support the individual.

- **Brain Development:** A process that begins twenty-one days after conception and continues until your last breath. Whether awake or asleep, for every second of your life brain development is occurring, typically without your assistance or participation. That does not mean we cannot intentionally participate and direct our brain's development. The *Your Faithful Brain* book/guidebook are both designed to assist and guide this intentionality in a way that is optimal, beginning with the commandments of Jesus to "love the Lord your God with all your heart, soul, mind, and strength, and love your neighbor as yourself." This is the optimal environment for brain development.

- **Corrective Emotions:** Powerful responses (guilt, sorrow, anxiety, and embarrassment) that we experience when our behaviors do not line up with our values. If we pay attention to these emotions, they can be the catalyst for change in our behaviors. We must be careful, however, lest corrective emotions such as self-loathing become corrosive and debilitating. These emotions say, "There is something wrong with me." Corrective emotions say, "There is something wrong with my behavior." Corrective emotions spur us to take responsibility, while corrosive emotions shut us down.

- **Emotional Salience:** What identifies a thought as being noticeable or prominent so that it is more likely to be made into a permanent memory. This applies to memories attached to experiences of both joy and sorrow. Through hippocampal rehearsal (the creation of your self-narrative), we can reduce the impact of negative memories and increase the impact of positive memories.

- **God's Created Reality:** A term coined by Dallas Willard and used in *Your Faithful Brain* to emphasize the fact that while each of us creates his or her own reality, none of us have *the* reality that God offers. A key aspect of healthy maturation is to do whatever we can to align with how God has designed us, others, and the world to work *best*.

- **Living intentionally:** The idea that our goals, values, and principles by which we live bring us into alignment with God's will for our lives. It means consistently structuring our choices and behaviors in such a way as to reflect our goals, values, and principles based on God's will. This provides an environment for optimal brain health and development.

For additional terminology from YFB and this guidebook, look in the index of Dr. Matheson's original text.

APPENDIX C

More than Quotes

Throughout *YFB* guidebook, you probably noticed we included several quotes and passages from other authors and books in addition to scriptural passages.

First, in terms of Scripture, within the pages of this book, we have used a variety of Bible translations and our choice in every cased depended on the topic and perspective we hoped to emphasize.

Personally, we want to share with you that both of us prefer having access to a variety of translations in order to help enrich our understanding of Scripture. There are times when each of us has experienced God's message a bit deeper depending on the translation we're reading.

When a certain passage sticks out or if one from within these pages stuck with you, we encourage you to look it up in a variety of translations and see if this enhances your experience of the passage. Try reading it out loud. Try writing it down. If you don't have a variety of translations handy, you can go online for a resource like http://Biblegateway.com and look up Scripture in several translations for free. But if you have the time and love to turn the physical pages like we do, there are many translations available to use at your local library.

We would love to hear how engaging Scripture this way enhances your experience of God and increases your understanding as well as application of His Word.

Next, we understand that not everyone has read the resources we have read nor do we all "travel in the same circle" as far as literature and research are concerned. So with that in mind, we created this appendix portion of the book to assist you in exploring more deeply the topics and ideas presented within these pages. These are topics and ideas we could only introduce by way of snippets and quotes, but we encourage you to delve deeper.

In this appendix, you will find a brief introduction to the original authors of the quotes, the main focus of their body of work and careers, and some additional resources created by them you may want to check out. In many cases, you will find our personal reflections on why we like a particular author or resource and how it has influenced our journey.

In certain instances, we will not be offering additional information. In most cases, this is only because some of those individuals quoted are people whom we have experienced in our own personal lives through seminars or TED Talks or some other genre in which no other additional information or resources are available. In some other cases, we did not expand on the author because their larger bodies of work aren't really applicable to the themes presented here.

We want to give a small disclaimer here as well. While we may not agree with everything each of these authors has to say, we do believe their work is important to our mission here. We strongly encourage you to look through the variety of books, articles, and additional resources each has to offer. We are confident there will be concepts from each individual's work that will further enhance your journey.

We suggest you use some of the resources here (if you find them pertinent to your journey) to create a new and expanded list of your own resources. This will help you intentionally build your full life.

You may use any of our resources, but we know the benefits firsthand of finding your own. Remember to look for them in a variety of areas and mediums like books, videos, teachings, songs, or anything else that speaks to you and inspires you to grow.

We hope you find the information in this appendix helpful and hope that it serves as an encouragement to continue the journey of developing *your* faithful brain.

1. *"The greatest discovery of my generation is that a human being can alter his life by altering his attitudes of mind."*—William James

   William James was an American philosopher and psychologist. He was also the first educator to offer a psychology course in the United States. His father was a prominent theologian (Henry James, Sr.). James, Jr. originally trained to be a physician but soon learned his passion was in philosophy and psychology.

   James is known as one of the leading thinkers of the late nineteenth century. He is also believed by many to be one of the most influential philosophers to ever come from the United States. Still, others have labeled him the "father of American psychology."

   His main interests were pragmatism, psychology, philosophy of religion, epistemology, and meaning of life. Jame's most important and influential books were *The Principles of Psychology* and *The Varieties of Religious Experiences*. James died in August 1910.

2. *"The kind of truth that makes us free is when our minds and our hearts begin to agree with God and we begin to see things the way He does. It re-makes us. It transforms us."*—Bob Hamp

   Bob Hamp is an international teacher, speaker, and author. Bob is also a Licensed Marriage and Family Therapist (LMFT) in the Dallas-Fort Worth area. He is a gifted communicator with a heart for helping people find freedom in Christ. One of the ways he does this is through free topical classes every Tuesday evening via Facebook Live from Think Differently Counseling, Consulting, Connecting. He is the author of the *Think Differently* series. The quote we used here is from his newly released (at the time of this writing) *Think Differently, Live Differently.*

3. *"Only in relationship with the other am I free."*—Dietrich Bonhoeffer

   Dietrich Bonhoeffer was an ordained minister and German pastor. He was a theologian and known for his intense resistance to Nazi dictatorship, for which he sacrificed his life. His writings on Christianity's role in the secular world have become widely influential. Consequently, his book, *The Cost of Discipleship,* has become a modern classic.

   While Bonhoeffer isn't widely known outside Christian circles, we believe his writings are important because of how he addresses our responsibility to humanity and to the world. One of our favorite quotes from Bonhoeffer, which didn't make it into our book, is as follows: *"We must learn to regard people less in light of what they do or omit to do, and more in the light of what they suffer."* A call for grace and mercy if ever we heard one.

   We highly recommend looking through his body of work to discover something that might speak to you. Dietrich Bonhoeffer died in a Nazi prison camp in April 1945.

4. *"Let's not be afraid to accept each day's surprise, whether it comes with joy or sorrow. It will open a new place in our hearts."*—Henri Nouwen

   Henri Nouwen was a Dutch Catholic priest, professor, writer, and theologian. Given that his interests were rooted primarily in psychology, pastoral ministry, spirituality, social justice, and community, it's probably plain to see why we wanted to include something from his extensive body of work.

   The real challenge was in choosing what quote to use!

Nouwen taught for just under twenty years at academic institutions, including the University of Notre Dame, Yale Divinity School, and Harvard Divinity School. He went on to work with individuals with intellectual and developmental disabilities at the L'Arche Daybreak Community in Richmond Hill, Ontario. He died in September 1996.

Perhaps our most loved piece of Nouwen's work is *The Inner Voice of Love*. He didn't write it originally with the intention of sharing; he wrote it for the sake of reflecting upon what he believed God was showing him about his own life. The more he shared it with those around him who were suffering, the more he was encouraged to publish it. And we're glad he did!

It is full of pearls of wisdom and encouragement for our journeys. It's as though Nouwen were a friend, offering some comfort and truth for the road ahead. We highly suggest this particular book and encourage you to look into other works by Nouwen.

5. *"We are created for joy. Not a weak and watery concept of joy that merely dilutes our sadness and pain. Rather, it is the hard deck on which all of life finds its legs; a byproduct of deeply connected relationships in which each member is consummately known."*—Curt Thompson

Curt Thompson is a psychiatrist who received his MD from Wright State University. He is also the author of *Anatomy of the Soul* and *The Soul of Shame*. Thompson is the consummate educator. As founder of the Center for Being Known, he and this nonprofit offer training and resources to educate and train leaders in the fields of mental health, education, business, and in the church with regard to how interpersonal neurobiology and Christian spiritual formation intersect.

We first learned of Thompson and his body of work when we were in grad school, pursuing our clinical training as mental health therapists. We feel his works are important in helping us understand relationships and how we're designed. His work is a gift to the exploration of faith and science as partners. We look forward to any additional works he offers.

6. *"God creates out of nothing. Wonderful you say. Yes, to be sure, but he does what is still more wonderful: he makes saints out of sinners."*—Søren Kierkegaard

   Søren Kierkegaard was a Danish philosopher, theologian, poet, social critic, and religious author. Many consider him to be the first existentialist philosopher. One of the reasons we chose to include him in our work is because of his important reflections on morality, ethics, psychology, and the philosophy of religion.

   Much of his philosophical work emphasizes concrete human reality over abstract thinking and highlights the importance of personal choice and commitment. As we're sure you've experienced by now, we place an important emphasis on personal agency and intentionality with regard to cultivating a life that is full and in line with God's created reality.

   We further appreciate Kierkegaard's theological focuses on Christian love. His psychological work, in which he explored the emotions and feelings of individuals when faced with life choices, is important to our understanding of self and others.

   Though Søren Kierkegaard died in November 1855, we find much of his work to be relevant today. His work can be challenging in many respects. We encourage you to explore his body of work and see if any titles pop out to you.

7. *"What gives me the most hope every day is God's grace; knowing that His grace is going to give me the strength for whatever I face, knowing that nothing is a surprise to God."*—Rick Warren

Rick Warren is the pastor of Saddleback Church in California. But he is also a *New York Times* bestselling author of *The Purpose Driven Life*, which has sold more than 30 million copies. His works have spawned countless conferences and endeavors in building and growing individuals, groups, and churches.

Each of us (Dondra, Gina, and Len) have at one time or another found a quote, study, concept, or teaching of Warren's to be relevant and helpful. Regardless of where you are in your faith journey, *The Purpose Driven Life* is a helpful tool in searching for the purpose and significance you're created for.

8. *"If we do not fill our minds with guilt and self-recriminations, we will recognize our incompleteness as a kind of spaciousness into which we can welcome the flow of grace."—Gerald G. May*

Gerald G. May was a psychiatrist and theologian as well as an author whose writing most often explored the combined ideas of spirituality and psychology, making him a certainty as a resource for our guidebook.

We have both personally found his work *Grace and Addiction* to be a powerful tool, not only in our work with clients and their family members, but also in our personal journeys. Upon closer examination, you will find that this particular piece of his work has a lot of value to all of us. Its benefits are not exclusive to those struggling with addiction alone.

May eventually joined the Shalem Institute for Spiritual Formation in Bethesda, Maryland, where he became a senior fellow conducting workshops in contemplative theology and psychology. He has written several books advancing the cause for combining spiritual direction with psychological treatment. Gerald G. May died in April 2005.

We highly encourage you to explore his body of work and are confident you will find a number of resources that will benefit you as you pursue growth and even healing, perhaps in areas you weren't even aware required it.

9. *"With God it's not about beholding life, but being held ourselves in the act of beholding it."—Craig D. Lounsbrough*

Craig D. Lounsbrough has been a counselor for over twenty-nine years in a variety of treatment settings, including psychiatric hospitals, outpatient clinics, facilities for the blind, churches, various ministries, and more. Additionally, Lounsbrough has ten years' experience in youth, associate, and senior pastoral roles.

He spent two years broadcasting in Christian radio and has published both nationally and internationally. He is a licensed professional counselor in Colorado, an ordained minister, and a certified professional life coach. This combination of talents and an understanding of Faith and Science make him a welcome addition to the resources we've drawn upon in writing this guidebook.

He has a variety of works available for counselors as well as individuals. We encourage you to explore his body of work and see if one is a fit for you and your unique journey.

10. *"Any man could, if he were so inclined, be the sculptor of his own brain."—Santiago Ramón y Cajal*

Santiago Ramón y Cajal is widely recognized in neuroscience as the preeminent neuroanatomist. As seen in the above quote, he is in all likelihood talking about the physical structure of the brain. Yet we know such a quote has deeper meaning. We believe he knew that as well.

He was a Spanish neuroscientist and pathologist who specialized in neuroanatomy. The central nervous system was a particular emphasis of his work. Santiago, along with Camillo Golgi, received the Nobel Prize in Physiology for Medicine in 1906, becoming the first person of Spanish origin who won a scientific Nobel Prize. Hundreds of his drawings illustrating the delicate arborizations of brain cells are still in use for educational and training purposes.

Although he died in October 1934, there is much to learn and be fascinated by in his work and in his drawings. The story of his life and how he became known in many circles as the "father of modern neuroscience" may be of interest to you as well.

11. *"Define yourself radically as one beloved by God. This is the true self. Every other identity is illusion."—Brennan Manning*

Brennan Manning is one of the most beloved authors, speakers, and teachers in our collection of contributors. While we love the quote above, the one he is possibly most famous for, and the one we would hope all those who subscribe to the Christian faith would remind themselves of daily, is the following:

"The greatest single cause of atheism in the world today is *Christians* who acknowledge *Jesus* with their lips and walk out the door and deny Him by their lifestyle. That is what an unbelieving world simply finds unbelievable."

His life story is one worth reading and can be found in snippets throughout his works on grace, truth, and love. He experienced firsthand the redeeming love and presence of God and spent his life helping others learn the same.

I (Gina) had the privilege of listening to and meeting Brennan in 2007 and was forever changed by his passion and authenticity. Sadly, Brennan died in 2013, but his beautiful truths and message live on in his body of work.

A couple favorites of ours are *The Ragamuffin Gospel* and *Abba's Child*. We recommend listening to or watching some videos of his teachings as well.

12. *"Grace isn't just forgiveness, it is forgiveness fueled by surrender."*—Amy E. Spiegel

    Amy E. Spiegel holds a degree in environmental political science. She seeks to shatter stereotypes and walk in faithfulness no matter the perception and encourages others to do the same. She is a Christ-follower and reflects this in her writings and work.

    Amy is also a speaker and writes weekly posts for http://WisdomAndFollyBlog.com. Additionally, she co-authors some projects with her husband, James Spiegel, about their family adventures. A fun work of theirs is titled *Gum, Geckos, and God*.

    We chose to include her because she really cares about cultivating the relationship that matters most. And let's face it, this quote of hers fits seamlessly in with the subject matter of our chapter in the guidebook.

13. *"Jesus tapped me on the shoulder and said, 'Bob, why are you resisting me?' I said, 'I'm not resisting You!' He said, 'You gonna follow Me?' I said, 'I've never thought about that before!' He said, 'When you're not following Me, you're resisting Me.'"*—Bob Dylan

    Bob Dylan is an American singer-songwriter, author, and artist who has been an influential figure in popular music and culture for more than five decades. He's . . . well, he's *Bob Dylan!*

14. *"Holding our story and loving ourselves through that process is the bravest thing we will ever do."*—Brené Brown

    Brené Brown is a research professor at the University of Houston who has spent much of her career studying courage, vulnerability, shame, and empathy. We have found her work to be very important in both our personal and professional lives.

While we recommend any of her work, our personal favorites are *I Thought It Was Just Me (but it isn't)*, *The Gifts of Imperfection*, and *Daring Greatly*. Perhaps these are our favorites because she speaks from a place of personal experience, not merely research and psychology. We learn a lot about what she has learned, and if we're paying attention, we'll learn a lot about her faith too.

If you are unfamiliar with her work, a great place to start is with her TED Talk on *The Power of Vulnerability*, which has over 30 million views.

15. *"The war against me and the war against you is about lies."*—Polly Wright-Hamp

   Polly Wright-Hamp is a speaker, teacher, and author. Among her many creative approaches to communication, she uses experiential art to help people in their journey to healing. Polly also leads workshops to help women heal from past traumas. Her passion to help individuals find freedom comes from her own journey. She's a certified NLP practitioner and practices in Grapevine, Texas. The above quote can be found in its entirety in the ACCEPT portion of Chapter 5. It is taken from Polly's book, *Cherished: Shattered Innocence. Restored Hope*. Polly cohosts the podcast *Can They Say That?* with me (Gina).

16. *"So take seriously the story God has given you to live. It's time to read your own life, because your story is the one that could set us all ablaze."* —Dan Allender

   Dan Allender received his MDiv from Westminster Theological Seminary and his PhD in counseling psychology from Michigan State University. He was part of our education during graduate school. We had the privilege of reading several of his references throughout our coursework.

We also participated in a nine-month program created and taught by Allender, aimed at training counselors in advanced trauma care. We had the privilege of being among the first to attend this course, which has grown into training for a variety of leaders and professionals who work with the hurting.

In his private practice, Dan's focus is on trauma recovery (particularly sexual abuse), story, and relationships. He is also a speaker and professor, training counselors to work with clients. Allender has authored a large body of work aimed at helping people grow and heal.

We encourage you to look into the resources he has to offer including seminars, lectures, podcast, and videos. A couple of our favorite books by Allender are *To Be Told: Know Your Story, Shape Your Future* and *The Healing Path*. However, we encourage you to look into his entire body of work and see what speaks to you.

17. *"…your history of silence won't do you any good, did you think it would? Let your words be anything but empty. Why don't you tell them the truth?"*—Sara Bareilles

   Sara Bareilles is most widely known as an American singer-songwriter. However, she's also a published author of her memoir *Sounds Like Me: My Life (So Far) In Song* and is known as a champion of women's rights and an advocate for women around the world.

   She has also written scores for Broadway and even won a Tony for her performance as Mary Magdalene in NBC's live adaptation of *Jesus Christ Superstar*.

   We find her music inspiring and, at times, anthem-like, particularly, her song "Brave," from which we took the above quote.

18. *"The way I see it, putting your faith in God is something that each person has gotta come to on his or her own. It's your own personal relationship with Him; a bond that is as unique as a fingerprint."—Bethany Hamilton*

    Bethany Hamilton is a professional surfer who survived a tragic shark attack in which her left arm was bitten off. She ultimately returned to surfing and has been winning competitions ever since. Bethany wrote about her experience in the 2004 autobiography *Soul Surfer: A True Story of Faith, Family, and Fighting to Get Back on the Board*. It became a feature film called *Soul Surfer* in April 2011.

    We have found her story to be one of inspiration and appreciate the vulnerability and authenticity from which she tells her story.

19. *"Go where your best prayers take you."—Frederick Buechner*

    Frederick Buechner is an American writer, whose writing spans a vast range of genres from poetry to fiction to autobiography. He is also a preacher and theologian. He is best known for his works *A Long Day's Dying* and *Godric*, a first-person narrative of the life of the medieval saint. His autobiographical works have been long quoted, particularly in spiritual works.

    Buechner has been described as "one of our most original storytellers" by *USA Today*. He also has authored some daily reflection books that may be helpful for your journey. We suggest taking a look at all he has to offer, as the collection is vast and discovering which one holds a description that fits where you are, or where you want to go next, in enhancing your life to the full.

20. *"Love is not the opposite of power. Love IS power. Love is the strongest power there is."—Vironika Tugaleva*

    Vironika Tugaleva is a Ukrainian-born author, speaker, and activist. Her desire to help people grow and heal came from her own journey of addiction, isolation, and a challenging past. While she speaks from a more "neutral" spiritual platform, she believes that spirituality is indeed important and that there is power within each of us to heal and grow.

She has left the ideals of traditional "self-help" behind, trading them in for a more organic and internal approach. We read and quote her with some cautions, but we find her helpful and entertaining. You may want to start with her blog or website to see if she's for you.

21. *"You have been woven together with great care, with intentionality, with skill and artistry and the occasional flair for the dramatic."*—Greg Holder

   Greg Holder is pastor of Len Matheson's home church, The Crossing, in Chesterfield, Missouri. He is the author of *The Genius of One*. He is also the cocreator of the Advent Conspiracy Movement. Dr. Matheson's original book, *Your Faithful Brain*, is dedicated to Greg. You can find his sermons available online.

22. *"To be loved but not known is comforting but superficial. To be known and not loved is our greatest fear. But to be fully known and truly loved is, well, a lot like being loved by God. It is what we need more than anything. It liberates us from pretense, humbles us out of our self-righteousness and fortifies us for any difficulty life can throw at us."*—Tim Keller

   Tim Keller is a pastor and theologian. He is what many refer to as a Christian apologist, meaning he speaks in defense of Christianity and helps people to see and debate the key tenets of the faith. One of our favorite books by Keller is The New York Times bestselling book, *The Prodigal God: Recovering the Heart of the Christian Faith*.

   You can find his sermons available through podcasts from Redeemer (the church he pastors in New York). One of our all-time favorites is *The Still Small Voice*. There are a variety of topics to choose from on the podcast. Browse and find something that stands out to you.

There are two additional works of his we find helpful to the Christian walk. They are *The Reason for God: Belief in an Age of Skepticism* and *Making Sense of God: An Invitation to the Skeptical*.

23. In the final chapter of this guidebook, we expand on the importance of healthy, loving relationships. In this section, we quote two authors, Sue Johnson and Susan Pinker, who have each done important work in the areas of loving relationships and their connection to our overall well-being.

    Sue Johnson is a PhD psychologist and recognized leader in the field of relational interventions. She is best known for her breakthrough clinical research using emotions in the therapy room to help shape secure, lasting bonds that create resilience. We highly recommend her book *Hold Me Tight* and its companion book *Created for Connection*.

    Susan Pinker is a psychologist, author, and social science columnist. Her work has been featured in *The Economist*, *The Financial Times*, and *Der Spiegel*. She draws on scores of psychological and sociological studies to bring us a concise and applicable approach to improving our quality of life. You can find her talk on the importance of a healthy social life on TED Talks. The book we quoted from is titled *The Village Effect: How Face-to-Face Contact Can Make Us Healthier and Happier*.

24. There is one last reference we made in our guidebook, which, while not a direct quote, deserves recognition in this appendix. And that's Aaron Beck.

    Aaron Beck is a psychiatrist, professor, and author of over 600 professional journal articles. He has influenced and been quoted in countless texts and has written or co-authored twenty-five books. He is regarded as the Father of Cognitive Therapy, and his theories are widely used in the treatment of clinical depression.

Beck has been named one of the "Americans in history who shaped the face of American psychiatry." His work has made an impact on us personally and professionally. There are a variety of therapies rooted in Cognitive Behavioral Therapy, and we've each watched our clients benefit from experiencing them. We couldn't complete this list of resources without recognizing the importance and influence of his work.

That's it! We wish we had all the time and space in the world to talk over books and resources with you, but for now, this will have to do.

Feel free to reach out to us if you are in need of more specific resources. If, through the work you've done in this guidebook, you have had the realization that you require some help on your journey, please reach out to us. If possible, we would love to help you find a qualified counselor in your area.

We hope you have found this additional list of information helpful and we look forward to hearing how it has enhanced your exploration and development of *your* faithful brain.

CONTACT INFORMATION

To share your experiences or find more ways to ignite heart-brain connection at the intersection of Faith and Science, visit us at:

http://www.faithfulbrain.com/guidebook

We would love to hear from you!

You can contact us at:

dondra@faithfulbrain.com

or

gina@faithfulbrain.com

Visit us for additional resources at:

www.faithfulbrain.com